Copyright © 2023 by Ethan J. Monroe (Author)

All rights reserved. No part of this book may be reproduced or utilized in any form or by any means, electronic or mechanical, including photocopying, recording or by any information storage and retrieval system, without permission in writing from the publisher, except for brief quotations in critical articles or reviews.

The content of this book is based on various sources and is intended for educational and entertainment purposes only. While the author has made every effort to ensure the accuracy, completeness, and reliability of the information provided, the information may be subject to errors, omissions, or inaccuracies. Therefore, the author makes no warranties, express or implied, regarding the content of this book.

Readers are advised to seek the guidance of a licensed professional before attempting any techniques or actions outlined in this book. The author is not responsible for any losses, damages, or injuries that may arise from the use of information contained within. The information provided in this book is not intended to be a substitute for professional advice, and readers should not rely solely on the information presented.

By reading this book, readers acknowledge that the author is not providing legal, financial, medical, or professional advice. Any reliance on the information contained in this book is solely at the reader's own risk.

Thank you for selecting this book as a valuable source of knowledge and inspiration. Our aim is to provide you with insights and information that will enrich your understanding and enhance your personal growth. We appreciate your decision to embark on this journey of discovery with us, and we hope that this book will exceed your expectations and leave a lasting impact on your life.

Title: Resilience Rising: Safeguarding Crypto's Future
Subtitle: Building a Trustworthy Ecosystem: Transparency and Security Measures

Series: Rugpulls Unveiled: Untangling the Web of Deceit in Early Crypto
Author: Ethan J. Monroe

Table of Contents

Introduction 7

Triumph Over Adversity: Celebrate the resilience of the crypto community in the face of rugpulls and scams. 7

Lessons from the Past: Reflect on the hard-earned wisdom and experiences that paved the way for a more secure future. 12

The Road Ahead: Set the stage for exploring how the crypto ecosystem evolved to combat rugpulls and protect investors. 17

Chapter 1: Building a Trustworthy Ecosystem 22

Transparency and Accountability: Investigate the importance of transparency and how projects embraced accountability to regain trust. 22

Enhanced Security Measures: Examine the advancements in security protocols to safeguard against hacks and exploits. 27

The Role of Auditing: Understand how independent audits became a crucial element in validating project integrity ... 32

Chapter 2: The Rise of Decentralized Governance. 37

Decentralized Decision-Making: Explore the emergence of decentralized governance models that empowered community participation. 37

Token Voting Mechanisms: Discuss how token holders gained influence in shaping project directions and deterring potential rugpulls. 43

The Challenges of Consensus: Delve into the complexities of achieving consensus in a decentralized environment. 48

Chapter 3: Strengthening Investor Protection 53

Investor Education: Highlight the importance of educating investors about risks and due diligence. 53

Investor Rights and Redress: Examine efforts to establish investor protections and avenues for redress in case of fraud...58

Escrow and Vesting: Discuss the implementation of escrow and vesting mechanisms to safeguard investor funds. 63

Chapter 4: Regulation and Compliance................. 68

A Shifting Landscape: Analyze how regulatory frameworks adapted to the rapidly evolving crypto space...................... 68

KYC and AML Measures: Explore the implementation of Know Your Customer (KYC) and Anti-Money Laundering (AML) practices in the crypto world. 73

Regulating Exchanges: Understand how regulations addressed the challenges posed by crypto exchanges. 78

Chapter 5: The Ethics of Freedom and Oversight .. 82

Striking the Balance: Examine the ethical debates surrounding the need for oversight and the preservation of decentralization. 82

Privacy Concerns: Discuss the tension between privacy rights and regulatory requirements in the crypto realm. ... 86

Code is Law: Explore the concept of "code is law" and its implications on governance and disputes. 90

Chapter 6: Global Perspectives on Regulation 94

Divergent Approaches: Compare how different countries and regions responded to regulating the crypto industry. 94

Regulatory Sandboxes: Analyze the concept of regulatory sandboxes and their role in fostering innovation while ensuring investor protection. 99

Collaboration and Convergence: Discuss the potential for international collaboration and standardization in crypto regulation. 104

Chapter 7: Evolving Together: Industry Collaboration 108

The Power of Collaboration: Explore how collaboration among projects and industry stakeholders promoted a safer environment. 108

Self-Regulatory Initiatives: Discuss how the crypto community took proactive steps to establish self-regulatory standards. 112

Uniting for a Brighter Future: Celebrate the collective efforts made to combat rugpulls and advance the crypto space..*116*

Conclusion **121**

The Journey of Resilience: Reflect on the transformation of the crypto ecosystem in the face of rugpulls. *121*

Empowering the Community: Emphasize the role of a proactive and informed community in safeguarding the crypto industry. *126*

A Roadmap for the Future: Propose a vision for a sustainable and secure crypto landscape, built on the lessons of "Resilience Rising." *131*

Wordbook **136**

Supplementary Materials **140**

Introduction

Triumph Over Adversity: Celebrate the resilience of the crypto community in the face of rugpulls and scams.

In the fast-paced and dynamic world of cryptocurrencies, the journey towards widespread adoption has been far from smooth. From its inception, the crypto landscape has been marred by instances of rugpulls and scams that threatened to undermine trust and stability. Yet, amidst these challenges, a remarkable story of resilience has emerged – a story of a community that refused to be deterred by setbacks, a community that chose to rise above adversity, learn from its mistakes, and forge a path toward a more secure future. This chapter celebrates the triumph of the crypto community over the adversities posed by rugpulls and scams, a journey that has reshaped the industry and its participants.

The Early Days: Navigating the Wild West

As cryptocurrencies gained popularity, the absence of regulatory oversight and the relative anonymity of transactions provided fertile ground for opportunistic fraudsters. In the absence of established norms and safeguards, unsuspecting investors fell victim to schemes that promised high returns but delivered devastating losses.

These early experiences laid the foundation for a community that would soon learn the importance of due diligence and education.

The Birth of Resilience: Learning from Mistakes

With each rugpull incident, the crypto community faced a unique test of its resilience. Rather than retreating in the face of adversity, community members and projects alike rallied together to address vulnerabilities, enhance security measures, and share hard-earned lessons. These experiences marked a turning point, igniting a commitment to building a more trustworthy ecosystem that would stand the test of time.

A Call for Transparency: From Shadows to Spotlight

In the aftermath of rugpulls, a resounding demand for transparency echoed across the crypto landscape. Projects that recognized the value of openness began sharing their development progress, financial status, and operational plans with their communities. This shift marked a departure from the secrecy that once shrouded the industry, paving the way for better-informed investors and fostering a sense of accountability among project teams.

The Emergence of Community Vigilance: Uniting Against Fraud

As rugpulls persisted, a spirit of collective vigilance took root within the community. Crypto enthusiasts became increasingly adept at spotting red flags, conducting thorough research, and questioning the legitimacy of projects. The shared experiences of being targeted by scams fostered a sense of camaraderie that transcended borders and languages, with individuals from around the world joining forces to protect one another.

A Catalyst for Innovation: Necessity Breeds Progress

The specter of rugpulls served as a powerful catalyst for innovation. Developers and security experts collaborated to devise advanced security protocols, robust smart contract auditing procedures, and decentralized governance models that shifted decision-making power away from a single entity. These innovations represented not only technical advancements but also a collective determination to prevent history from repeating itself.

Educating for Empowerment: Empowering Investors Against Fraud

Education emerged as a cornerstone of the crypto community's response to rugpulls. Newcomers and seasoned investors alike sought out information on how to assess projects, evaluate risks, and protect their investments. The rise of online resources, communities, and educational initiatives not only empowered investors to make informed decisions but also fortified the industry against malicious actors.

Embracing Diversity: A Global Network of Resilience

The resilience exhibited by the crypto community in the face of rugpulls transcended borders, cultures, and ideologies. From the bustling metropolises to the remote corners of the world, a network of individuals connected by a shared passion for cryptocurrencies emerged. This diversity became a source of strength, as different perspectives converged to shape a more inclusive and resilient industry.

A New Era of Collaboration: Forging a Safer Future

The triumph over rugpulls was not the endpoint of the crypto community's journey but the beginning of a new chapter. Through collaboration, transparency, and vigilance, the community harnessed the lessons learned to foster an environment that values security and accountability. As the crypto landscape evolved, so did the collective determination to safeguard the investments and aspirations of those who believed in the transformative potential of blockchain technology.

In the pages that follow, we delve deeper into the intricate tapestry of this remarkable journey. From the emergence of decentralized governance to the evolution of global regulations, we explore the strategies, innovations, and challenges that defined the crypto community's response to rugpulls. Through this exploration, we come to understand not only the industry's resilience but also its unwavering commitment to shaping a future where the potential of cryptocurrencies can be fully realized – a future built on the foundation of "Resilience Rising."

Lessons from the Past: Reflect on the hard-earned wisdom and experiences that paved the way for a more secure future.

In the ever-evolving landscape of cryptocurrencies, lessons learned from the past serve as invaluable guideposts on the journey to a more secure and resilient future. The crypto community's ability to adapt, learn, and innovate in the face of adversity has transformed the industry's trajectory. This chapter delves deep into the profound insights gained from historical rugpull incidents and scams, exploring how these experiences have catalyzed a paradigm shift in the approach towards security, transparency, and governance.

Understanding the Cost of Ignorance: The Early Days of Vulnerability

In the early days of cryptocurrencies, the allure of rapid wealth creation often blinded both investors and project creators to the potential risks. The lack of proper due diligence and the absence of regulatory oversight led to an environment where bad actors could thrive. The consequences of this era of innocence were felt by countless individuals who fell victim to scams and rugpulls, resulting in financial losses and eroded trust.

Translating Pain into Progress: Embracing a Culture of Accountability

As the crypto community confronted the fallout from rugpulls, a fundamental shift in mindset occurred. Instead of dwelling on the losses, individuals and projects turned their pain into a catalyst for change. They recognized that a lack of accountability was at the heart of the problem and that transparency was the key to rebuilding trust. This realization laid the groundwork for a new culture of accountability, where project teams acknowledged mistakes, engaged in open dialogue with their communities, and took proactive measures to rectify errors.

Security as a Non-Negotiable Priority: The Rise of Resilience

The repeated breaches of security highlighted a dire need for innovation in the field of cybersecurity. The hard-earned lessons from these breaches compelled developers, white-hat hackers, and security experts to collaborate on enhancing the robustness of blockchain networks and smart contracts. The crypto community transitioned from a reactive stance to a proactive one, placing security at the forefront of technological advancements.

Empowering the Investor: The Importance of Education

Rugpull incidents exposed the knowledge gap that existed among investors, many of whom lacked the understanding needed to assess the credibility of projects. The harsh consequences of this knowledge deficit prompted a renewed commitment to investor education. Various platforms, communities, and experts emerged to provide resources that empowered investors with the tools to make informed decisions, fostering a more resilient and vigilant investor base.

Decentralized Governance: Lessons from the Wisdom of Crowds

Rugpull incidents underscored the vulnerability of centralized decision-making. The projects that emerged from the ashes of these incidents embraced the principle of decentralized governance, recognizing that involving the community in decision-making processes could prevent the concentration of power and mitigate the risk of abuse. The crypto community drew inspiration from these experiences to craft governance models that put power back into the hands of the people.

The Regulation Conundrum: Striking a Balance

In the aftermath of rugpulls, regulatory bodies around the world grappled with how best to balance innovation and investor protection. The lessons learned from these incidents prompted a nuanced conversation about the role of regulation in the crypto landscape. While excessive regulation could stifle innovation, a lack of regulation could leave investors vulnerable. The crypto community learned to advocate for balanced and thoughtful regulatory approaches that fostered growth while safeguarding interests.

Collaboration Beyond Boundaries: A Global Response

Rugpull incidents transcended geographical boundaries, affecting individuals and projects across the world. This shared experience sparked an unprecedented level of cross-border collaboration. Crypto enthusiasts, developers, regulators, and thought leaders from different regions came together to share insights and best practices. These interactions enriched the global crypto ecosystem with diverse perspectives and approaches to tackling common challenges.

From Victimhood to Victory: The Transformation of Resilience

The crypto community's journey from victimhood to victory serves as a testament to the power of resilience. The scars left by rugpulls and scams are not merely reminders of past mistakes but symbols of growth and evolution. They have paved the way for a more secure, transparent, and inclusive crypto landscape. The lessons learned from adversity have transformed vulnerabilities into strengths, creating a foundation upon which the future of cryptocurrencies can be built with greater confidence.

As we delve into the subsequent chapters, we will examine how these hard-earned lessons have been applied to shape the crypto industry's trajectory. From transparency initiatives to investor education programs, each step taken represents a deliberate response to the challenges faced in the past. By reflecting on the wisdom distilled from these experiences, we lay the groundwork for a crypto future that thrives on resilience, empowerment, and innovation.

The Road Ahead: Set the stage for exploring how the crypto ecosystem evolved to combat rugpulls and protect investors.

The crypto industry's journey has been one of continuous adaptation and evolution. As the technology matured, so did the strategies and solutions employed to combat the persistent threat of rugpulls and scams. This chapter sets the stage for our exploration of the transformative measures that have reshaped the crypto ecosystem, ensuring a more secure and investor-friendly environment. From the emergence of advanced security protocols to the evolution of regulatory frameworks, we delve into the landscape that emerged from the ashes of adversity.

Embracing the Challenge: An Industry in Flux

The emergence of rugpulls and scams cast a shadow over the crypto industry, compelling stakeholders to confront the vulnerabilities that existed within the ecosystem. The community's response was not one of defeat but of determination. By acknowledging the challenges and embracing them as opportunities for growth, the industry set the tone for a series of changes that would redefine its trajectory.

A Technological Renaissance: Advancements in Security Protocols

The crypto landscape responded to the threat of rugpulls with a surge of technological innovation. Developers, engineers, and cybersecurity experts collaborated to create advanced security protocols that fortified blockchain networks and smart contracts. Multi-signature wallets, threshold cryptography, and bug bounty programs emerged as essential tools in the fight against breaches, reflecting a shift towards a more proactive and resilient approach to security.

Transparency as a Shield: Auditing and Accountability

One of the cornerstones of the industry's transformation was the recognition that transparency was paramount in rebuilding trust. Independent auditing emerged as a critical practice, providing an external validation of project integrity. Auditors scrutinized smart contracts, reviewed code, and assessed financial disclosures to ensure alignment with project goals and community expectations. This emphasis on accountability paved the way for projects to earn back the confidence of investors.

Decentralized Governance: Empowering the Community

The rise of decentralized governance models marked a significant turning point in the fight against rugpulls. Projects recognized that empowering the community to participate in decision-making processes not only mitigated the risk of centralization but also fostered a sense of shared responsibility. Token voting mechanisms and proposal systems transformed passive investors into active participants, effectively deterring malicious actors and reinforcing project legitimacy.

Knowledge as Armor: Investor Education and Empowerment

In the aftermath of rugpulls, the industry pivoted towards educating and empowering investors. Resources, webinars, and educational platforms emerged to equip investors with the knowledge needed to navigate the complexities of the crypto landscape. Armed with a better understanding of project evaluation, risk assessment, and due diligence, investors became more discerning and resilient, reducing the likelihood of falling victim to fraudulent schemes.

The Regulatory Renaissance: Balancing Innovation and Protection

Regulatory bodies responded to the challenges posed by rugpulls by striving to strike a delicate balance between fostering innovation and safeguarding investors. Regulatory frameworks evolved to incorporate the unique characteristics of the crypto industry while ensuring measures to prevent fraud and abuse. The crypto community's proactive engagement with regulators facilitated a more collaborative approach that aimed to protect participants without stifling innovation.

Ethics and Privacy: Navigating a Complex Landscape

As the industry matured, ethical considerations took center stage. The tension between the principles of decentralization and the need for oversight prompted thoughtful debates. The concept of "code is law" faced scrutiny as the crypto community grappled with finding a harmonious equilibrium between privacy rights, regulatory compliance, and ethical responsibilities. This dialogue laid the groundwork for a more nuanced and inclusive approach to governance.

Global Synchrony: Collaborative Initiatives and Standardization

The challenges posed by rugpulls transcended national borders, fostering a spirit of international collaboration. Regulatory sandboxes, cross-border initiatives, and intergovernmental cooperation emerged as mechanisms for fostering innovation while ensuring investor protection. The industry's collective pursuit of standardization across regions showcased a commitment to creating a unified and secure global crypto landscape.

The Quest for Sustainability: A Vision Realized

The road ahead for the crypto ecosystem is paved with the footsteps of resilience, innovation, and adaptability. The industry's evolution from a vulnerable playground to a secure and investor-friendly environment is a testament to the commitment of countless individuals who refused to let adversity define the narrative. The crypto industry stands on the threshold of a future where lessons from the past have shaped a landscape that is not only more resilient but also more inclusive, ethical, and ready to fulfill its transformative potential.

As we embark on our journey through the chapters that follow, we will dive deep into the strategies, initiatives, and collaborative efforts that have fortified the crypto industry against rugpulls and scams. From regulatory frameworks to decentralized governance models, each milestone represents a deliberate step toward a future where the lessons learned and the wisdom gained illuminate the path to a more secure and promising crypto landscape.

Chapter 1: Building a Trustworthy Ecosystem
Transparency and Accountability: Investigate the importance of transparency and how projects embraced accountability to regain trust.

In the wake of rugpulls and scams that shook the foundations of the crypto industry, the concept of transparency emerged as a beacon of hope—a means to rebuild trust and foster a culture of accountability. This chapter delves into the pivotal role of transparency and accountability in reshaping the crypto ecosystem. It explores how projects, communities, and stakeholders came to recognize that open and honest communication was not just a best practice but a prerequisite for establishing a trustworthy environment.

Transparency as a Paradigm Shift: The Awakening

The age of rugpulls exposed the vulnerabilities inherent in an ecosystem that had grown too quickly for its own good. Projects that once operated in the shadows, guarded by veils of secrecy, were now under intense scrutiny. The realization dawned that transparency was not merely an option but a fundamental pillar for fostering trust and preventing the recurrence of fraudulent activities. This realization marked a profound paradigm shift, prompting projects to revisit their operational practices.

Opening the Books: Financial Transparency and Disclosures

One of the cornerstones of transparency lay in the realm of financial disclosures. In the past, projects had often concealed their financial status, sowing seeds of doubt among investors. The road to redemption began with projects adopting open-book policies, providing detailed breakdowns of funds allocation, expenditure, and revenue streams. These disclosures served as a testament to financial integrity and gave investors the assurance they sought.

Beyond Lip Service: Demonstrating Development Progress

In a landscape where technology was paramount, demonstrating consistent development progress became essential. The industry recognized that showcasing real milestones and deliverables was more than a marketing strategy—it was a commitment to transparency. Projects embraced regular progress reports, showcasing advancements, code updates, and feature releases. This practice ensured that investors and the broader community could track a project's trajectory, fostering an atmosphere of credibility.

The New Face of Communication: Open Dialogue and Community Engagement

The era of rugpulls underscored the importance of maintaining open lines of communication with the community. Projects that once operated with minimal interaction began to embrace community engagement as a means to rebuild bridges. Regular AMA (Ask Me Anything) sessions, town hall meetings, and interactive forums allowed community members to voice concerns, ask questions, and contribute to decision-making processes. This newfound collaboration solidified the notion that transparency was a two-way street.

From Oversight to Self-Policing: Building Mutual Trust

Transparency extended beyond projects to encompass the broader industry. Initiatives like project rating platforms, independent audits, and community-driven assessments empowered investors to make informed decisions. This shift from reliance on centralized authority to a decentralized web of accountability was pivotal. Investors became co-guardians of the industry's integrity, and projects recognized the value of cultivating mutual trust with their supporters.

Navigating Ethical Dilemmas: Addressing Challenges Head-On

Transparency demanded confronting ethical dilemmas head-on. Projects acknowledged the challenges, ranging from tough decisions about token burns to managing community expectations. By transparently communicating the reasoning behind these decisions, projects sought to build understanding and empathy within the community. The willingness to engage with difficult conversations marked a departure from the past and laid the foundation for a more mature industry.

A Return to Trust: Rebuilding Confidence

The crypto community's collective response to rugpulls was not just about establishing transparency for the sake of optics—it was about rebuilding confidence in a technology that had the power to transform industries. As projects embraced transparency and demonstrated accountability, they began to witness the gradual restoration of trust. Investors who had once been wary were now becoming cautiously optimistic, recognizing that transparency was the cornerstone upon which lasting relationships were built.

Transparency Beyond Today: A Pillar for the Future

The journey towards transparency and accountability was not a short-term fix but a commitment to a lasting transformation. It was a pledge to uphold values that would shape the industry's trajectory for years to come. As projects continued to demonstrate their dedication to transparency, they helped pave the way for a more resilient and investor-friendly crypto ecosystem. The lessons learned through transparency had far-reaching implications, influencing not only individual projects but the very fabric of the industry itself.

    In the chapters that follow, we delve into other vital aspects of building a trustworthy crypto ecosystem. From enhanced security measures to the role of auditing in validating project integrity, we explore how the industry harnessed these lessons to construct a resilient foundation. The journey of transparency and accountability is an ongoing narrative—one that weaves its way through the industry's evolution, guiding its transformation into a space that values integrity, openness, and a commitment to a safer future.

Enhanced Security Measures: Examine the advancements in security protocols to safeguard against hacks and exploits.

The crypto landscape, once marred by vulnerabilities that emboldened malicious actors, underwent a significant transformation in response to the threat of rugpulls and scams. This chapter delves into the advancements in security protocols that emerged as a response to these challenges. From the development of sophisticated encryption techniques to the evolution of smart contract audits, the crypto industry harnessed technological innovation to fortify its defenses and create a more secure ecosystem.

The Vulnerability Conundrum: Understanding the Nature of Threats

The rise of rugpulls and scams highlighted the vulnerabilities that lurked within the crypto landscape. Exploits ranged from basic code vulnerabilities to complex attacks that took advantage of smart contract flaws. This realization forced the industry to acknowledge that security was not a luxury but a necessity. As a result, the crypto community embarked on a journey to understand the nature of threats and to develop comprehensive strategies for mitigating risks.

Encryption as a Shield: Safeguarding Data and Transactions

A pivotal aspect of security lay in the encryption of data and transactions. Cryptography, long a cornerstone of the crypto industry, evolved into a formidable shield against malicious intent. Projects embraced end-to-end encryption to protect user communications and transactional data from prying eyes. This step not only preserved privacy but also bolstered trust in the security of the ecosystem.

Smart Contract Audits: Navigating the Complexities of Code

Smart contracts, while revolutionary, introduced a new layer of complexity and vulnerability. Projects recognized the importance of thorough code reviews and audits to identify potential vulnerabilities before they could be exploited. Professional auditing firms, specialized in blockchain security, emerged to scrutinize smart contracts for vulnerabilities, ensuring that projects delivered secure and robust code to their users.

Bug Bounties and White-Hat Collaboration: Harnessing the Community's Expertise

Recognizing that even the most thorough audits might miss certain vulnerabilities, projects embraced a collaborative approach. Bug bounty programs invited ethical hackers—often referred to as white-hat hackers—to search for vulnerabilities in exchange for rewards. This practice leveraged the collective knowledge of the community to identify and rectify potential security gaps before they could be exploited for malicious purposes.

Multi-Signature Wallets: Distributing Access for Enhanced Security

As the industry evolved, the concept of multi-signature wallets gained prominence. Unlike traditional wallets, which relied on a single private key, multi-signature wallets required multiple authorized signatures to initiate transactions. This approach reduced the risk of unauthorized access and provided an additional layer of security, making it significantly harder for malicious actors to compromise user funds.

Immutable vs. Upgradeable Contracts: Balancing Security and Flexibility

The debate between immutable and upgradeable smart contracts underscored the delicate balance between security and flexibility. While immutable contracts ensured that code remained unchanged, they posed challenges if vulnerabilities were discovered post-deployment. On the other hand, upgradeable contracts provided the ability to fix vulnerabilities but introduced risks of centralization. Projects grappled with these considerations, seeking solutions that maintained security without sacrificing adaptability.

Zero-Knowledge Proofs and Privacy: Enhancing Transaction Confidentiality

The crypto industry also explored zero-knowledge proofs and privacy-focused technologies to enhance the confidentiality of transactions. Zero-knowledge proofs allowed users to prove the validity of a statement without revealing any specific information. This innovation had implications for privacy-focused projects and applications, offering a way to conduct transactions with a higher degree of anonymity.

Decentralized Identity and Self-Sovereign Identity: Empowering Users

Enhanced security measures extended beyond transactions and code to include user identity. Decentralized identity solutions, often referred to as self-sovereign identity, allowed users to have greater control over their personal information. By using blockchain to verify identity attributes, users could authenticate themselves without relying on centralized entities, reducing the risk of identity theft and fraud.

The Ever-Evolving Landscape: A Dynamic Defense

The quest for enhanced security measures marked an ongoing journey, not a destination. The crypto industry understood that threats would continue to evolve, requiring constant vigilance and innovation. The advances made in security protocols reflected the community's commitment to maintaining the integrity of the ecosystem. As projects embraced encryption, auditing, collaboration, and cutting-edge technologies, they fortified their defenses, ensuring that the industry's future would be shaped by resilience rather than vulnerability.

The subsequent chapters delve into other crucial aspects of building a trustworthy crypto ecosystem. From the role of independent audits in validating project integrity to the emergence of decentralized governance models, we explore how the industry harnessed these advancements to create a foundation of resilience and security. The journey toward safeguarding the crypto landscape was not without challenges, but through the dedication to innovation, the industry laid the groundwork for a more secure future.

The Role of Auditing: Understand how independent audits became a crucial element in validating project integrity.

In the aftermath of rugpulls and scams that eroded trust in the crypto industry, a pressing need emerged for a mechanism that could validate the integrity of projects. Independent audits, once relegated to the realm of traditional finance, rose to prominence as a critical tool for rebuilding confidence and ensuring transparency. This chapter delves into the pivotal role that auditing played in reshaping the crypto ecosystem, shedding light on how it transformed from a novel concept into an indispensable practice.

The Genesis of Skepticism: The Need for Objective Validation

As rugpull incidents continued to expose vulnerabilities in project design and execution, investors grew increasingly skeptical of the industry's claims. Promises of groundbreaking technology and transformative products were no longer sufficient to assuage concerns. The need for objective, third-party validation became evident—a validation that would not only confirm the veracity of claims but also restore faith in projects and their teams.

Bringing Traditional Finance to the Blockchain: Auditing Redefined

Auditing, a concept firmly entrenched in traditional finance, was transplanted into the realm of cryptocurrencies. Projects recognized that independent audits had the potential to bridge the trust gap, offering investors assurance that a project's code, financials, and operations were being scrutinized by unbiased experts. This shift marked a profound transformation—an industry embracing a practice once deemed incompatible with its decentralized ethos.

The Anatomy of an Audit: Processes and Procedures

Independent audits underwent an adaptation process to suit the unique characteristics of the crypto industry. Auditors navigated complex codebases, evaluated smart contract logic, and verified financial transactions. The meticulous process aimed to identify vulnerabilities, assess financial stability, and ensure adherence to project roadmaps. This comprehensive evaluation served as a litmus test for project credibility.

A New Breed of Experts: Blockchain Auditors

The specialized nature of crypto projects demanded auditors with an intricate understanding of blockchain technology and smart contract intricacies. Blockchain auditors emerged as a new breed of experts, armed with the technical prowess to dissect code for potential vulnerabilities and the analytical skills to evaluate project whitepapers for feasibility. Their role went beyond mere scrutiny—it was an essential element in the validation of project integrity.

Building Trust Through Transparency: Audit Reports

The output of an independent audit came in the form of a comprehensive report that detailed findings, identified risks, and recommended remedial actions. These reports were more than technical documents; they were a testament to a project's commitment to transparency. By sharing audit results with the public, projects not only demonstrated their willingness to be held accountable but also empowered investors with the information needed to make informed decisions.

From Skepticism to Assurance: The Investor Perspective

The adoption of independent audits had a profound impact on investor sentiment. Skeptical investors, once hesitant to commit funds, began to see audited projects as a safer bet. The assurance provided by audit reports mitigated the risk of potential rugpulls or scams, making the decision to invest a more informed one. This change in perception underscored the transformational effect of audits on project credibility.

The Ripple Effect: Industry-Wide Adoption

As the benefits of independent audits became apparent, their adoption snowballed throughout the industry. Projects that previously eschewed audits began to realize the advantages of third-party validation. Auditing firms expanded their reach, offering services tailored to the needs of blockchain projects. This industry-wide adoption marked a turning point—an acknowledgment that audits were not just a passing trend but a fundamental practice.

The Challenge of Limited Resources: Accessibility and Scalability

Despite the benefits, some projects faced challenges in accessing audit services. Smaller projects or those with limited resources found audits to be cost-prohibitive. This prompted discussions about scalability and accessibility, driving efforts to create more inclusive audit solutions. Collaborative initiatives and community-driven assessments emerged as alternatives, ensuring that even projects with modest means could undertake some form of validation.

The Road Ahead: Continuous Improvement and Innovation

The role of independent audits did not culminate in a static practice but rather marked the beginning of a continuous cycle of improvement and innovation. As the crypto landscape evolves, auditors adapt their methodologies to address emerging threats and vulnerabilities. The lessons learned from audits contribute to the industry's collective wisdom, fostering an environment that values accountability, transparency, and investor protection.

As we navigate through the subsequent chapters, we delve into other crucial components of building a trustworthy crypto ecosystem. From transparency initiatives to investor education, each facet interconnects to create a foundation that is fortified against the threat of rugpulls. The evolution of auditing, from an unconventional idea to an industry standard, underscores the crypto industry's resilience and determination to learn from its past and construct a safer and more secure future.

Chapter 2: The Rise of Decentralized Governance

Decentralized Decision-Making: Explore the emergence of decentralized governance models that empowered community participation.

In response to the vulnerabilities exposed by rugpulls and scams, a paradigm shift took place within the crypto community. The emergence of decentralized governance models marked a departure from traditional top-down decision-making structures and ushered in an era of inclusivity, empowerment, and community-driven innovation. This chapter delves into the evolution of decentralized governance, its impact on project sustainability, and how it empowered community members to actively shape the future of the crypto ecosystem.

The Catalyst for Change: Addressing the Limitations of Centralization

The centralized nature of many crypto projects came under scrutiny in the wake of rugpulls. A single point of control not only concentrated power but also left projects vulnerable to manipulation or misuse. The need for a more democratic and inclusive approach to decision-making became evident. The advent of decentralized governance served as a response to these concerns, transforming the power dynamics between project teams and their communities.

A Paradigm of Participation: Redefining Governance

Decentralized governance represented a radical departure from conventional models. Instead of decisions being made exclusively by project founders or developers, power was distributed across token holders. This shift acknowledged that the collective wisdom of a diverse community was better equipped to steer projects toward success, fostering an environment where ideas were evaluated on merit rather than hierarchy.

Token Voting Mechanisms: A Voice for Every Holder

Token voting mechanisms emerged as the cornerstone of decentralized governance. Token holders were empowered with the ability to cast votes on proposals that determined project directions, feature implementations, and resource allocation. This mechanism gave even the smallest holders a voice, ensuring that decisions were reflective of the broader community's sentiment rather than the interests of a select few.

Evolving Governance Structures: From DAOs to Futarchy

The evolution of decentralized governance gave rise to a spectrum of models, each with its own unique characteristics and implications. Decentralized Autonomous Organizations (DAOs) took center stage, allowing projects to operate with a degree of autonomy while being steered by community proposals. Futarchy, a model that uses prediction markets to guide decision-making, showcased the industry's willingness to experiment with innovative governance structures.

Navigating Complexity: Challenges of Consensus

While decentralized governance offered promising benefits, it was not without its challenges. Achieving consensus within a diverse and global community proved to be intricate. The crypto community grappled with questions of voter apathy, governance token distribution, and the potential for manipulation. Over time, projects experimented with mechanisms to incentivize participation and strike a balance between direct democracy and practical decision-making.

Decentralized Governance in Practice: Success Stories and Lessons Learned

Numerous projects embraced decentralized governance, each showcasing unique approaches and outcomes. Projects like MakerDAO and Compound demonstrated the power of token-based decision-making, allowing their communities to influence protocol parameters and ensure stability. These success stories illustrated that when wielded responsibly, decentralized governance could foster innovation, adaptability, and a sense of ownership among community members.

The Promise of Longevity: Sustainability Through Community Involvement

Decentralized governance was not just a response to rugpulls; it was a strategy for long-term project sustainability. By involving the community in decision-making, projects forged a deep sense of loyalty and commitment among token holders. This commitment extended beyond the immediate aftermath of rugpulls, transforming token holders into project stewards invested in the project's success over the long haul.

The Balancing Act: Navigating Community Versus Development

While community-driven decision-making was a hallmark of decentralized governance, projects had to navigate a delicate balance between community input and efficient development. The challenge lay in incorporating the desires of the community while ensuring the project's technical and strategic integrity. This tension prompted discussions about the extent to which developers should follow community guidance.

A Holistic Vision: Integrating Governance and Sustainability

Decentralized governance extended beyond mere decision-making—it was a testament to a holistic vision for the industry. It combined technological innovation, social cohesion, and economic alignment into a single framework. Projects recognized that fostering a thriving ecosystem required more than code; it demanded the active involvement of a diverse and engaged community.

The Road Ahead: Continuous Refinement and Exploration

The emergence of decentralized governance models marked a transformative phase in the crypto industry's journey. As projects continue to refine their governance structures and experiment with new models, the industry inches closer to a future where decisions are shaped collectively by those with a stake in the ecosystem. Decentralized governance is not just a buzzword—it is a tangible manifestation of the industry's evolution toward greater inclusivity, transparency, and resilience.

The subsequent chapters dive into other pivotal aspects of building a trustworthy crypto ecosystem. From strengthening investor protection to examining regulatory frameworks, each topic is interwoven into the broader narrative of how the industry responded to rugpulls and scams. The evolution of decentralized governance stands as a testament to the industry's commitment to empowering its participants and forging a path toward a more secure and community-driven future.

Token Voting Mechanisms: Discuss how token holders gained influence in shaping project directions and deterring potential rugpulls.

In the wake of rugpulls and scams that shook the trust in centralized decision-making, the crypto community sought to redefine the governance landscape. The rise of token voting mechanisms heralded a new era of decentralized decision-making, where token holders gained a direct say in shaping project directions and mitigating the risk of potential rugpulls. This chapter delves into the evolution of token voting mechanisms, their impact on project governance, and how they transformed the relationship between projects and their communities.

Token Holders as Stakeholders: A Fundamental Shift

Token holders, once passive investors, became active stakeholders through token voting mechanisms. These mechanisms granted token holders the power to propose, evaluate, and vote on proposals that dictated the trajectory of projects. The shift was profound, transforming token holders from mere financial supporters to influential participants in the project's governance and development.

A Voice for the Community: Fostering Inclusivity

Token voting mechanisms democratized governance, ensuring that every token holder had a voice. The size of a holder's stake determined the weight of their vote, creating an egalitarian system that considered both the quantity of tokens held and the sentiment of individual stakeholders. This inclusivity countered the risk of centralization and promoted diverse perspectives, allowing projects to tap into the collective wisdom of their communities.

Project Evolution Through Token Votes: Examples of Impact

The impact of token voting was evident in numerous projects that embraced this model. Proposals spanned from technical upgrades to strategic shifts, ranging from introducing new features to modifying economic parameters. Notable projects like Uniswap and Aave empowered token holders to influence liquidity pool rewards and fee structures, enabling them to actively shape the protocols they were invested in.

Deterring Potential Rugpulls: A Collective Safeguard

One of the significant contributions of token voting mechanisms was the enhanced ability to deter potential rugpulls and scams. Transparent and community-driven decision-making mitigated the risks associated with centralized control. Token holders could voice concerns, demand clarifications, and even vote against proposals that appeared suspicious. This mechanism created an environment where malicious actors faced increased scrutiny and resistance.

Enforcing Accountability: Governance as a Check and Balance

Token voting mechanisms introduced an inherent accountability framework. Project teams had to align with the interests of their community to ensure proposals received support. This accountability extended to the management of project funds, as token holders could vote against misappropriation or excessive expenditures. The result was a system where transparency, integrity, and alignment with community values became prerequisites for successful governance.

Challenges of Token Voting: Addressing Concerns

While token voting mechanisms offered promising benefits, they were not without challenges. Voter apathy, disproportionate influence of large token holders, and the potential for governance attacks were concerns that needed to be addressed. Projects experimented with strategies such as quadratic voting to counterbalance the influence of large holders and create a more equitable decision-making process.

From Decisions to Culture: The Ripple Effect

The impact of token voting extended beyond decision-making; it permeated the culture of projects. The inclusivity fostered by these mechanisms created a sense of ownership among token holders. As the community's influence grew, projects adopted a more collaborative approach, acknowledging that the collective intelligence of stakeholders could drive innovation, enhance project sustainability, and ultimately contribute to deterring rugpulls.

Governance Token Value: Aligning Incentives

Token voting mechanisms aligned the value of governance tokens with the success of the project. Positive governance outcomes translated into increased investor confidence, potentially driving up the value of tokens. This alignment of incentives ensured that token holders were not just voting for their preferences but were actively contributing to the project's growth and long-term success.

A Stepping Stone to a New Paradigm: Lessons and Potential

Token voting mechanisms marked a stepping stone toward a new paradigm of governance. The lessons learned from the successes and challenges of these mechanisms laid the foundation for further innovation. Projects explored hybrid governance models, experiments with quadratic funding, and improvements in on-chain governance interfaces. This evolution highlighted the dynamic nature of the crypto industry and its relentless pursuit of refining decentralized governance.

The Ongoing Experiment: Building a Decentralized Future

As we delve deeper into the chapters that follow, we uncover more layers of the industry's response to rugpulls. From strengthening investor protection to exploring regulatory frameworks, each facet contributes to the industry's transformation. The emergence of token voting mechanisms is a testament to the industry's adaptability and its commitment to forging a path where transparency, collaboration, and decentralized decision-making create a more secure and resilient crypto ecosystem.

The Challenges of Consensus: Delve into the complexities of achieving consensus in a decentralized environment.

The emergence of decentralized governance models brought with it the promise of inclusivity, transparency, and community-driven decision-making. However, beneath the surface of these ideals lay a myriad of challenges associated with achieving consensus in a decentralized environment. This chapter delves into the complexities that projects faced as they navigated the path to agreement, the diverse approaches employed to address these challenges, and the lessons learned from the pursuit of consensus within a decentralized framework.

Decentralization as a Double-Edged Sword: The Struggle for Consensus

Decentralization, while empowering, presented a paradoxical challenge when it came to achieving consensus. Unlike traditional centralized structures where a single authority could impose decisions, decentralized governance relied on the collective agreement of diverse stakeholders. The inherent diversity of opinions, priorities, and visions often created tension, requiring innovative solutions to foster agreement while maintaining the essence of decentralization.

Token Holder Participation: The Quest for Engagement

One of the primary challenges of achieving consensus was encouraging meaningful participation from token holders. While token voting mechanisms provided the tools for decision-making, low voter turnout or apathy among holders could undermine the legitimacy of outcomes. Projects grappled with strategies to incentivize engagement, exploring mechanisms such as governance rewards, token-based incentives, and staking mechanisms to motivate active participation.

The Tyranny of the Majority: Addressing Power Imbalances

Decentralized governance brought with it the risk of power imbalances. Large token holders could potentially sway decisions in their favor, leaving smaller stakeholders marginalized. The challenge lay in striking a balance between the influence of those with significant stakes and ensuring that minority voices were not drowned out. Projects sought mechanisms to limit the dominance of large holders while respecting their contributions.

Synergy Amidst Diversity: Navigating Conflicting Interests

The diverse nature of the crypto community meant that stakeholders often had conflicting interests and priorities. Striking a harmonious balance between different stakeholder groups, each with its vision for project development, required careful navigation. Projects experimented with mechanisms that enabled compromise and negotiated solutions, fostering a collaborative environment where diverse perspectives could coalesce.

The Speed of Decision-Making: Balancing Deliberation and Agility

Decentralized decision-making could sometimes be slower compared to centralized models due to the necessity of consensus-building. While thorough deliberation was essential, the pace of technological development demanded agility. Striking the right balance between careful consideration and timely execution was a challenge that projects faced, prompting discussions on efficiency, decision thresholds, and emergency decision-making mechanisms.

Avoiding Governance Attacks: The Need for Security

Decentralized governance also introduced the challenge of governance attacks—manipulative efforts to hijack decision-making processes. Malicious actors could exploit vulnerabilities in governance mechanisms to push through proposals that benefited them at the expense of the community. Ensuring the security and robustness of governance systems was paramount to prevent such attacks and maintain the integrity of decision-making.

The Role of Education and Transparency: Overcoming Misinformation

Effective consensus-building required clear communication and transparency. Misinformation or misunderstanding about proposals could hinder the ability to reach agreement. Projects recognized the importance of educating token holders about the implications of decisions, providing detailed information, and fostering open dialogue to ensure that decisions were made based on accurate and well-informed perspectives.

Experiments in Decision-Making Models: Learning from Iteration

The pursuit of consensus in a decentralized environment was an iterative process. Projects experimented with various decision-making models, adjusting parameters, thresholds, and mechanisms in response to challenges and community feedback. The lessons learned from these experiments informed the industry's collective understanding of what worked best within the context of decentralized governance.

The Promise of a Consensus-Driven Future: Learning and Adapting

As we progress through the chapters ahead, we continue to explore the multifaceted response of the crypto industry to rugpulls and scams. From strengthening investor protection to navigating regulatory landscapes, each aspect contributes to the transformation of the ecosystem. The challenges of achieving consensus in a decentralized environment highlight the industry's resilience, adaptability, and commitment to learning and adapting as it strives to create a more secure, inclusive, and consensus-driven future.

Chapter 3: Strengthening Investor Protection
Investor Education: Highlight the importance of educating investors about risks and due diligence.

In the aftermath of rugpulls and scams, the crypto industry recognized that empowering investors with knowledge was paramount to fostering a safer and more resilient ecosystem. The rise of investor education initiatives marked a shift from a climate of uninformed speculation to one of informed decision-making. This chapter delves into the significance of investor education, its role in preventing rugpulls, and the multifaceted approach taken to equip investors with the tools they needed to navigate the crypto landscape wisely.

The Dark Side of Ignorance: The Risk of Uninformed Investing

Rugpulls often thrived in an environment where investors lacked a fundamental understanding of the technology, risks, and dynamics of the crypto industry. Uninformed investments led to rash decisions, susceptibility to scams, and the unintentional support of fraudulent projects. The need for investor education became evident—a call to arm investors with the knowledge required to navigate this complex and rapidly evolving space.

Knowledge is Empowerment: The Foundation of Informed Decisions

Investor education aimed to empower individuals by equipping them with a comprehensive understanding of blockchain technology, project fundamentals, and risk assessment. By offering insights into the mechanics of cryptocurrencies, smart contracts, and decentralized finance (DeFi), investors could make informed decisions that aligned with their risk tolerance and financial goals.

The Role of Transparency: Dissecting Whitepapers and Roadmaps

Central to investor education was the dissection of project whitepapers and roadmaps. These documents served as windows into a project's intentions, technology, and business models. By providing guidance on how to scrutinize these materials, investor education helped individuals distinguish between projects with substantive foundations and those built on hollow promises.

Risk Assessment and Due Diligence: Navigating the Minefield

Investor education emphasized the importance of thorough due diligence. This process involved researching project teams, evaluating technical viability, assessing market demand, and understanding token economics. By equipping investors with a checklist for evaluating projects, education initiatives empowered them to make informed decisions grounded in facts rather than speculation.

Recognizing Red Flags: Identifying Potential Scams

Rugpulls and scams often exhibited common warning signs that could be discerned with a discerning eye. Investor education highlighted these red flags, ranging from promises of unrealistic returns to lack of transparent communication from project teams. By fostering a culture of skepticism and critical thinking, education initiatives enabled investors to spot potential scams before falling victim.

The Role of Regulatory Awareness: Navigating Legal and Compliance Aspects

Investor education extended beyond technical and project-related matters to include regulatory awareness. Understanding the legal landscape, compliance requirements, and potential risks associated with investing in the crypto industry became an essential aspect of informed decision-making. Education initiatives shed light on the importance of adhering to Know Your Customer (KYC) and Anti-Money Laundering (AML) practices.

Learning from Past Mistakes: Case Studies as Teaching Tools

Investor education drew lessons from past rugpulls and scams, turning them into valuable teaching tools. By analyzing historical incidents, education initiatives showcased how signs of trouble could have been detected earlier, and how risk mitigation strategies could have been employed. These case studies underscored the real-world implications of uninformed investing and served as cautionary tales.

From Webinars to Workshops: The Spectrum of Education Initiatives

Investor education initiatives spanned a spectrum of formats, from webinars and online courses to in-person workshops and educational resources. These initiatives were tailored to cater to both novice investors seeking to understand the basics and experienced traders looking to deepen their knowledge. By offering various avenues for learning, the industry aimed to reach a wide range of individuals.

A Cultural Shift: Fostering Responsible Investing

Investor education was not just about imparting knowledge; it was about fostering a cultural shift toward responsible investing. By equipping investors with the tools to evaluate projects critically, education initiatives sought to create a community that prioritized research, due diligence, and informed decisions over the allure of quick gains.

The Road Ahead: A Better-Informed Future

As we delve into the chapters that follow, we explore the industry's multifaceted response to rugpulls and scams. From strengthening investor protection to examining regulatory frameworks, each aspect contributes to the transformation of the ecosystem. The emphasis on investor education reflects the industry's commitment to equipping individuals with the skills and knowledge they need to participate responsibly and confidently in the crypto landscape, ultimately contributing to a more secure and resilient future.

Investor Rights and Redress: Examine efforts to establish investor protections and avenues for redress in case of fraud.

The crypto industry's growth brought both innovation and challenges, with investor protections and mechanisms for redress emerging as critical focal points in response to rugpulls and scams. This chapter delves into the evolution of investor rights and the establishment of avenues for redress in the event of fraud. From community-driven initiatives to regulatory frameworks, we explore how the industry aimed to create a safer environment for investors while preserving the ethos of decentralization.

The Need for Investor Protections: Bridging the Trust Gap

Rugpulls and scams exposed the vulnerabilities of investors in the decentralized landscape. The absence of traditional financial institutions meant that investors lacked established mechanisms for protection and recourse. The industry recognized that establishing investor protections was not only essential for investor confidence but also for the long-term sustainability of the crypto ecosystem.

Empowering Investors: Recognizing Their Rights

The journey toward investor protections began with the recognition of investor rights. Projects and industry stakeholders acknowledged that investors had the right to transparency, accurate information, and a safe investment environment. This acknowledgment marked a shift from a laissez-faire approach to one that embraced accountability and responsibility for the well-being of investors.

Community-Driven Initiatives: Self-Regulation in Action

In the absence of formal regulatory structures, the crypto community initiated self-regulation efforts to protect investors. Codes of conduct, community-driven audits, and guidelines for project transparency were developed to set standards for responsible behavior. These initiatives demonstrated the industry's proactive stance in fostering a culture of investor protection.

The Role of Regulatory Frameworks: Balancing Innovation and Security

While self-regulation played a role, formal regulatory frameworks emerged to provide a structured approach to investor protection. Regulatory bodies recognized the unique characteristics of the crypto industry and sought to strike a balance between fostering innovation and safeguarding investor interests. These frameworks introduced accountability measures, compliance requirements, and avenues for redress.

Know Your Customer (KYC) and Anti-Money Laundering (AML): Balancing Privacy and Accountability

Regulatory frameworks introduced practices such as Know Your Customer (KYC) and Anti-Money Laundering (AML) to identify and verify the identities of investors. While these practices aimed to mitigate risks and deter fraudulent activities, they also raised debates about privacy and the preservation of the pseudonymous nature of cryptocurrencies. Striking the right balance between privacy and accountability became a challenge.

Strengthening Legal Protections: Contracts and Dispute Resolution

The emergence of smart contracts brought a new dimension to investor protections. Projects began implementing contract terms that outlined investor rights, project commitments, and mechanisms for dispute resolution. These self-executing agreements aimed to provide a structured framework for addressing conflicts and holding parties accountable.

Creating Avenues for Redress: Escrow and Vesting Mechanisms

To protect investors from rugpulls and premature project exits, escrow and vesting mechanisms gained prominence. These mechanisms ensured that project teams could not access all funds immediately, reducing the risk of fraudulent actions. Vesting periods aligned incentives between investors and project teams, fostering long-term commitment and shared objectives.

The Role of Decentralized Autonomous Organizations (DAOs): Community Governance as Redress

Decentralized Autonomous Organizations (DAOs) provided an avenue for redress by enabling token holders to vote on proposals and decisions that affected the project. In cases of suspected fraud or mismanagement, token holders could propose and vote on measures to rectify the situation, ensuring that the community had a say in protecting its interests.

Building Bridges: Collaboration Between Projects and Investors

Investor protections and redress mechanisms were not just about regulatory compliance; they were about fostering healthy relationships between projects and their investors. Clear communication, regular updates, and transparent reporting built trust and ensured that investors had the information they needed to make informed decisions and take action in case of fraud.

The Ongoing Evolution: Striving for Investor Confidence

As we continue to explore the industry's response to rugpulls and scams in the chapters ahead, we dive into different facets of the transformation. From regulatory frameworks to ethical considerations, each aspect contributes to building a more secure crypto ecosystem. The establishment of investor protections and avenues for redress signifies the industry's commitment to fostering investor confidence while embracing the decentralized ethos that underpins the crypto revolution.

Escrow and Vesting: Discuss the implementation of escrow and vesting mechanisms to safeguard investor funds.

In the wake of rugpulls and scams that eroded investor trust, the crypto industry recognized the need for innovative mechanisms to protect investor funds. Escrow and vesting emerged as key tools to ensure that funds were safeguarded, project teams remained committed, and potential rugpulls were deterred. This chapter delves into the intricacies of escrow and vesting mechanisms, their role in strengthening investor protection, and the ways they reshaped the dynamics between project teams and their backers.

A Paradigm Shift in Fund Management: The Rise of Escrow and Vesting

Traditional financial models often allowed immediate access to funds, potentially exposing investors to the risk of rugpulls. Escrow and vesting mechanisms redefined fund management by introducing time-based release schedules that aligned incentives between project teams and investors. These mechanisms ensured that funds were used responsibly and that project teams remained committed to their stated objectives.

Escrow: A Safeguard Against Premature Access

Escrow mechanisms acted as a buffer against abrupt access to investor funds. In this arrangement, a third party, often a trusted entity or smart contract, held the funds and released them according to predefined conditions. Escrow mechanisms protected investors from immediate fund access and reduced the possibility of project teams disappearing with the funds.

Vesting: Aligning Incentives for Long-Term Commitment

Vesting mechanisms introduced a time-based release schedule for project teams and founders. Instead of receiving all funds upfront, they received funds incrementally over a predetermined period. Vesting ensured that project teams remained committed to their projects' development and success, as their financial incentives were tied to the project's longevity and achievement of milestones.

Deterring Rugpulls: The Economic Rationale

The implementation of escrow and vesting mechanisms had a direct impact on deterring rugpulls and scams. For project teams, the prospect of immediate access to funds was replaced with a more gradual and accountable release, discouraging any fraudulent intentions. Investors were reassured that project teams' financial motivations were aligned with the project's success, reducing the risk of rugpulls.

Tailoring Vesting Schedules: Balancing Rigor and Flexibility

The design of vesting schedules required careful consideration. Longer vesting periods ensured long-term commitment, but they could also create liquidity challenges for project teams. Striking the right balance between rigorous vesting and providing flexibility for project development was a delicate challenge, with no one-size-fits-all solution.

Community Trust and Transparency: Demonstrating Commitment

The adoption of escrow and vesting mechanisms was not just about protecting funds; it was about building trust within the community. Project teams that voluntarily subjected their funds to escrow and vesting demonstrated their commitment to the project's success. This transparency reassured investors that their financial contributions were in capable and responsible hands.

Escrow and Vesting as Industry Norms: A Paradigm Shift

As the adoption of escrow and vesting mechanisms gained momentum, they became industry norms rather than exceptions. Projects that did not embrace these mechanisms often faced skepticism and hesitation from investors. The standards set by these mechanisms contributed to reshaping investor expectations and bolstering investor confidence.

Challenges and Considerations: Customization and Adaptation

While escrow and vesting mechanisms offered significant benefits, their implementation was not without challenges. The customization of these mechanisms to suit project-specific needs, navigating legal complexities, and addressing the balance between project development and fund accessibility were aspects that required careful consideration and adaptation.

Vesting for Token Holders: Extending the Model

The concept of vesting was not limited to project teams and founders; it also extended to token holders. Some projects introduced vesting periods for tokens held by community members, aligning incentives and encouraging long-term participation. This extension of the vesting model aimed to foster a sense of commitment and shared ownership among token holders.

A New Era of Investor Protection: Escrow and Vesting in Practice

The implementation of escrow and vesting mechanisms marked a new era of investor protection within the crypto industry. These mechanisms embodied a commitment to accountability, responsibility, and long-term project sustainability. As we continue to explore the industry's multifaceted response to rugpulls in the chapters ahead, we uncover the various dimensions that contribute to building a more secure, transparent, and resilient crypto ecosystem.

Chapter 4: Regulation and Compliance

A Shifting Landscape: Analyze how regulatory frameworks adapted to the rapidly evolving crypto space.

The intersection of blockchain technology and cryptocurrencies with traditional financial systems presented regulators with an unprecedented challenge. As rugpulls and scams underscored the need for investor protection, regulatory frameworks needed to adapt to the rapidly evolving crypto space. This chapter delves into the dynamic evolution of regulatory approaches, the motivations behind these adaptations, and the impact on investor confidence and industry development.

The Emergence of a New Asset Class: Regulatory Conundrums

Cryptocurrencies introduced a new asset class that did not neatly fit within existing regulatory definitions. Regulators grappled with classifying cryptocurrencies as securities, commodities, currencies, or something entirely novel. This classification carried profound implications for taxation, investor protections, and market oversight.

Initial Coin Offerings (ICOs) and the Regulatory Dilemma

The rise of Initial Coin Offerings (ICOs) presented regulators with a unique challenge. ICOs enabled projects to raise funds through token sales, blurring the lines between fundraising and investment. Regulators had to navigate the tension between enabling innovation and safeguarding investors from potential scams or fraudulent offerings.

From Caution to Collaboration: Regulatory Responses

Initial regulatory responses to the crypto space often leaned towards caution and warnings about the risks involved. However, as the industry matured and sought legitimacy, a trend towards collaboration and dialogue between regulators and industry stakeholders emerged. Regulators realized that working with the industry was more effective in achieving balanced outcomes.

The Evolution of Regulatory Approaches: A Global Mosaic

Regulatory approaches varied significantly across different jurisdictions. Some countries embraced a welcoming stance, viewing cryptocurrencies as drivers of innovation, while others adopted more restrictive measures to mitigate risks. The diversity of approaches highlighted the complexity of the regulatory landscape and the challenge of achieving global harmonization.

A Patchwork of Guidance: Navigating Uncertainty

The lack of standardized regulations led to a patchwork of guidance that often left industry participants in a state of uncertainty. Projects had to grapple with jurisdictional nuances, compliance requirements, and shifting regulatory priorities. This uncertainty posed challenges for cross-border operations and international collaboration.

Seeking Clarity: Regulatory Sandboxes and Pilots

In response to the need for more clarity, regulatory sandboxes and pilot programs were established in various jurisdictions. These frameworks allowed projects to operate under regulatory supervision while testing their models in a controlled environment. Sandboxes enabled regulators to gather insights and tailor regulations to the industry's unique characteristics.

Anti-Money Laundering (AML) and Know Your Customer (KYC) Measures: Balancing Privacy and Compliance

Regulators aimed to address concerns around money laundering and illicit activities in the crypto space. Implementing Anti-Money Laundering (AML) and Know Your Customer (KYC) measures became essential for ensuring compliance. However, striking the right balance between privacy and regulatory requirements remained a challenge, sparking discussions on preserving the pseudonymous nature of cryptocurrencies.

Market Integrity and Investor Protection: Focus Areas for Regulation

As rugpulls and scams highlighted the vulnerabilities of the crypto market, regulators increasingly focused on market integrity and investor protection. Strengthening rules around trading practices, market manipulation, and fraudulent activities became priorities to ensure a level playing field and maintain investor confidence.

Regulatory Innovation: Tailoring Regulations to the Crypto Landscape

Traditional regulatory frameworks were not always well-suited to the dynamic and borderless nature of the crypto industry. Regulatory innovation became essential to address these gaps. Concepts such as "technology-neutral" regulations and principles-based approaches were explored to ensure regulations remained adaptable and relevant.

The Path Forward: Collaborative Regulation for a Secure Future

As we delve into the chapters ahead, we continue to explore the industry's response to rugpulls and scams. From enhancing investor protections to considering ethical dimensions, each facet contributes to the transformation of the ecosystem. The dynamic adaptation of regulatory frameworks reflects the industry's pursuit of a secure, innovative, and collaborative future—one that balances the benefits of decentralization with the need for responsible oversight.

KYC and AML Measures: Explore the implementation of Know Your Customer (KYC) and Anti-Money Laundering (AML) practices in the crypto world.

The rapid growth of the cryptocurrency industry brought with it unprecedented opportunities but also raised concerns about illicit activities and money laundering. As a response to these challenges, Know Your Customer (KYC) and Anti-Money Laundering (AML) measures were introduced to the crypto world. This chapter delves into the significance of KYC and AML practices, their implementation in the crypto ecosystem, and the impact they had on both industry integrity and investor protection.

Cryptocurrency's Double-Edged Nature: Innovation and Risks

Cryptocurrencies offered novel financial solutions and global accessibility, but their pseudonymous nature also made them attractive to those seeking to evade traditional financial oversight. This dual nature of cryptocurrencies highlighted the need to balance innovation with measures to prevent illegal activities.

The Foundation of AML and KYC: Understanding the Basics

Anti-Money Laundering (AML) regulations require institutions to implement measures to detect and prevent money laundering and terrorist financing. Know Your Customer (KYC) procedures involve verifying the identities of customers to ensure they are not engaging in illegal activities. These measures, common in traditional finance, were adapted to the crypto industry to maintain market integrity.

The Challenges of Pseudonymity: Striving for Transparency

Cryptocurrencies' pseudonymous nature posed a challenge for AML and KYC efforts. While offering privacy benefits, this anonymity also made it difficult to identify and track individuals engaging in suspicious transactions. Implementing AML and KYC in the crypto world required striking a balance between privacy rights and the need for financial transparency.

The Role of Exchanges: Gatekeepers to Compliance

Cryptocurrency exchanges became pivotal in implementing AML and KYC measures. As intermediaries between fiat currencies and cryptocurrencies, exchanges played a crucial role in ensuring that funds entering and leaving the crypto ecosystem complied with regulatory standards. They introduced customer verification processes and transaction monitoring to identify potentially illicit activities.

Enhancing Due Diligence: The KYC Process

The KYC process involved collecting and verifying customer information, such as identification documents and proof of address. Projects and exchanges implemented tiered verification levels, enabling users to access different services based on the level of information provided. This tiered approach aimed to strike a balance between compliance and user experience.

Transaction Monitoring: Detecting Suspicious Activities

AML measures involved monitoring transactions for patterns that could indicate money laundering or other illicit activities. The use of advanced algorithms and software helped exchanges identify unusual behavior, such as large or rapid transfers, which could be indicative of fraudulent intentions.

Challenges of Global Compliance: Navigating Jurisdictional Differences

The global nature of the crypto industry meant that AML and KYC practices had to be adapted to different regulatory environments. Cryptocurrency projects and exchanges had to navigate a complex web of regulations that varied from country to country, requiring robust systems to ensure compliance across multiple jurisdictions.

Decentralization vs. Compliance: Finding Common Ground

The implementation of AML and KYC practices raised questions about the compatibility of regulatory compliance with the ethos of decentralization. Some argued that these measures contradicted the ideals of privacy and financial sovereignty that underpinned cryptocurrencies. Striking a balance between these ideals and the need for regulatory compliance became a point of contention.

The Road to AMLD5 and FATF Guidelines: Industry Collaboration and Regulation

The international financial community recognized the need for consistent AML and KYC practices across borders. Initiatives such as the European Union's AMLD5 and the Financial Action Task Force (FATF) guidelines provided a framework for implementing AML and KYC measures in the crypto industry. These standards aimed to prevent money laundering, terrorist financing, and other illicit activities.

Impact on Investor Protection: Fostering Confidence

While some questioned the impact of AML and KYC measures on privacy, these practices also fostered investor confidence. Investors were reassured that exchanges and projects were taking steps to prevent fraudulent activities, thereby enhancing market integrity and protecting their investments.

The Ongoing Evolution: Balancing Privacy and Security

As we continue to explore the industry's response to rugpulls and scams in the chapters ahead, we delve into different facets of the transformation. From strengthening investor protection to examining ethical considerations, each aspect contributes to building a more secure, transparent, and resilient crypto ecosystem. The implementation of AML and KYC practices reflects the industry's ongoing effort to balance privacy and security while participating responsibly in the global financial landscape.

Regulating Exchanges: Understand how regulations addressed the challenges posed by crypto exchanges.

The rapid growth of the cryptocurrency industry led to the emergence of numerous cryptocurrency exchanges, acting as the gateways between the traditional financial system and the crypto ecosystem. However, this growth also raised concerns about investor protection, market integrity, and the potential for fraudulent activities. In response, regulatory frameworks were developed to address the challenges posed by crypto exchanges. This chapter explores how regulations aimed to create a secure and transparent environment for users while fostering innovation in the exchange sector.

The Pioneers of Crypto Exchanges: A New Frontier

The early days of cryptocurrency exchanges were marked by innovation and the pursuit of decentralized principles. However, the absence of clear regulatory guidelines led to a lack of uniform standards, contributing to concerns about security breaches, market manipulation, and scams.

The Quest for Market Integrity: Regulatory Oversight

The rapid proliferation of exchanges highlighted the need for regulatory oversight to ensure market integrity and prevent fraudulent activities. Regulatory bodies recognized that a lack of oversight could lead to an environment where investors were susceptible to rugpulls, hacks, and Ponzi schemes.

Addressing Security Concerns: Safeguarding User Funds

Security breaches and hacks posed significant risks to both exchanges and their users. Regulatory frameworks introduced security standards and guidelines that exchanges were required to adhere to. Measures included secure storage practices, multi-factor authentication, and regular security audits to protect user funds from theft.

Market Surveillance and Anti-Manipulation Measures

Regulators sought to prevent market manipulation and ensure fair trading practices. Exchanges were required to implement surveillance systems to detect suspicious trading activities. The goal was to create a level playing field for all participants and reduce the potential for price manipulation.

Licensing and Registration: Establishing Credibility

Regulatory frameworks introduced licensing and registration requirements for exchanges, establishing a layer of credibility and accountability. Exchanges were required to adhere to certain standards and undergo thorough assessments to prove their commitment to regulatory compliance and user protection.

Customer Protections: Safeguarding User Rights

To enhance customer protections, regulations required exchanges to establish clear terms of service, customer support mechanisms, and dispute resolution procedures. These measures aimed to ensure that users' rights were upheld and that they had avenues for redress in case of disputes.

AML and KYC Compliance: Preventing Illicit Activities

Regulatory standards around Anti-Money Laundering (AML) and Know Your Customer (KYC) procedures were extended to exchanges to prevent the use of cryptocurrencies for illicit activities. Exchanges were required to implement identity verification processes to ensure that transactions were traceable and compliant with legal standards.

Transparency and Disclosure: Building Trust

Regulations promoted transparency in the operations of exchanges. Exchanges were required to disclose information about their ownership, security practices, fee structures, and trading volumes. This transparency aimed to build trust among users and provide them with the information needed to make informed decisions.

Ensuring Liquidity: Balancing Innovation and Risk

While regulatory oversight aimed to protect users, it also had to balance the need for innovation and market development. Overly stringent regulations could stifle competition and limit the growth of the exchange sector. Regulators aimed to strike a balance that encouraged innovation while ensuring user safety.

Global Collaboration: Harmonizing Standards

As the cryptocurrency industry transcended national borders, regulatory bodies around the world recognized the need for global collaboration to address the challenges posed by exchanges. Initiatives such as the International Organization of Securities Commissions (IOSCO) provided a platform for regulators to exchange information and establish common principles.

An Evolving Landscape: Navigating Challenges

The crypto exchange landscape continued to evolve as regulatory frameworks adapted to new challenges. As we explore the industry's response to rugpulls and scams in the chapters ahead, we uncover the multifaceted transformation that aims to create a more secure and resilient crypto ecosystem. The regulation of exchanges plays a vital role in fostering trust, innovation, and responsible participation in the global financial landscape.

Chapter 5: The Ethics of Freedom and Oversight

Striking the Balance: Examine the ethical debates surrounding the need for oversight and the preservation of decentralization.

The emergence of cryptocurrencies brought to the forefront a fundamental ethical debate that continues to shape the evolution of the industry: how to balance the necessity for regulatory oversight with the principles of decentralization and individual freedoms. This chapter delves into the complex ethical considerations surrounding this debate, exploring the tension between regulatory safeguards and the preservation of the core values that underpin the crypto revolution.

Decentralization: A Paradigm of Freedom

At the heart of the cryptocurrency movement is the principle of decentralization—a departure from traditional financial systems dominated by central authorities. This ethos promises greater individual sovereignty over financial transactions, data, and information. Decentralization champions the idea that people should have control over their own assets without intermediaries and the potential for censorship.

Regulatory Oversight: A Response to Challenges

Rugpulls, scams, and illicit activities within the crypto space raised concerns about investor protection, market integrity, and financial stability. In response, regulatory oversight was deemed necessary to ensure compliance with laws, prevent fraudulent activities, and uphold the interests of both investors and society at large.

The Ethical Dilemma: Preservation vs. Regulation

The ethical debate revolves around striking a balance between preserving the ideals of decentralization and embracing the need for regulatory oversight. Advocates of decentralization argue that it empowers individuals and promotes financial inclusion. Critics of oversight worry that excessive regulation could stifle innovation and compromise individual freedoms.

Individual Privacy vs. Regulatory Scrutiny

One of the core ethical concerns lies in the tension between individual privacy and the need for regulatory scrutiny. Decentralization promises pseudonymity and privacy, but regulators argue that anonymity could enable illegal activities. Striking a balance between personal privacy and the demands of law enforcement raises complex questions about where the line should be drawn.

Censorship Resistance vs. AML/KYC Compliance

The concept of censorship resistance, central to decentralization, stands in contrast to Anti-Money Laundering (AML) and Know Your Customer (KYC) compliance requirements. Advocates of decentralization argue that these measures compromise the pseudonymous nature of cryptocurrencies, while proponents of oversight emphasize the importance of preventing money laundering and illicit activities.

Innovation vs. Investor Protection

Decentralization has been a driving force behind innovative financial solutions, but critics worry that unchecked innovation could lead to systemic risks and harm investors. Striking a balance requires ensuring that innovative ideas are nurtured while protecting the public from potential pitfalls.

Community Autonomy vs. Regulatory Authority

Decentralized communities have the autonomy to make decisions through consensus mechanisms, empowering participants to shape project directions. The introduction of regulatory oversight challenges this autonomy, prompting discussions about how to maintain community-driven decision-making while complying with legal requirements.

Global Coordination vs. Jurisdictional Diversity

The global nature of the crypto industry complicates the ethical debate. The challenge lies in finding common ground across jurisdictions with diverse regulatory approaches. Striving for global coordination raises questions about cultural differences, legal traditions, and the need to ensure that standards are adaptable to unique contexts.

Balancing the Scales: Pragmatic Solutions

Finding solutions that respect both the principles of decentralization and the need for regulatory oversight requires pragmatic thinking. Collaborative efforts between industry stakeholders, regulators, and policymakers become essential to bridge the divide and create frameworks that encourage responsible innovation without compromising ethical considerations.

A Vision for the Future: Harmonizing Ethics and Innovation

As we delve into the chapters ahead, exploring the industry's multifaceted response to rugpulls and scams, we continue to grapple with the ethical dimensions of freedom and oversight. By engaging in open dialogues, embracing technological advancements, and considering the broader societal implications, the crypto industry can navigate these ethical challenges and forge a path towards a more secure, transparent, and ethically sound future.

Privacy Concerns: Discuss the tension between privacy rights and regulatory requirements in the crypto realm.

The rise of cryptocurrencies has ignited a fierce debate surrounding the delicate balance between individual privacy rights and the regulatory imperatives aimed at safeguarding against illicit activities. This chapter delves into the complex landscape of privacy concerns within the crypto realm, examining the ethical and legal challenges posed by the tension between the promise of privacy and the demands of regulatory oversight.

The Pseudonymous Nature of Cryptocurrencies: A Double-Edged Sword

Cryptocurrencies, often touted as tools for financial freedom, offer a level of pseudonymity that traditional financial systems do not. This feature allows users to conduct transactions without revealing their real-world identities, providing a powerful shield against unwarranted intrusion into personal financial matters.

Privacy as a Human Right: An Ethical Imperative

Privacy has long been considered a fundamental human right. The ability to control one's personal information is seen as essential to maintaining autonomy, dignity, and freedom. The advent of cryptocurrencies further extends this notion by granting individuals greater control over their financial data.

The Dark Side of Anonymity: Illicit Activities and Regulatory Concerns

While privacy is championed as a cornerstone of cryptocurrencies, it has also been exploited for nefarious purposes. The pseudonymous nature of transactions has raised concerns about money laundering, terrorism financing, tax evasion, and other illicit activities that can thrive in the shadows.

Regulatory Requirements: The Need for Accountability

Regulatory bodies argue that privacy-focused cryptocurrencies could provide a haven for criminal activities, potentially undermining national security and financial stability. To mitigate these risks, governments worldwide have introduced Anti-Money Laundering (AML) and Know Your Customer (KYC) regulations that demand greater transparency in financial transactions.

The Conundrum of Anonymity vs. Accountability

The tension between privacy rights and regulatory requirements lies at the heart of the privacy conundrum. Cryptocurrency advocates argue that mandatory identification contradicts the very principles that underlie digital assets, eroding the foundational promise of pseudonymity.

Decentralization's Dilemma: Centralized Compliance Mechanisms

The challenge intensifies when considering that centralized exchanges are often required to implement KYC and AML procedures. This requirement runs counter to the decentralized ethos, as centralization for compliance undermines the very concept of individual control and empowerment.

Emerging Solutions: Privacy-Preserving Technologies

In response to the challenges, innovative privacy-preserving technologies have emerged. Zero-knowledge proofs, ring signatures, and confidential transactions enable transactions to remain private while still being verifiable and compliant with regulatory requirements.

Legal and Regulatory Perspectives: Jurisdictional Variations

Jurisdictional variations in privacy and financial regulations compound the complexities. Different countries have different expectations and standards for privacy protection, leading to a fractured global landscape in terms of both privacy rights and regulatory compliance.

Ethical Considerations: Finding Common Ground

The ethical dimension of the privacy debate weighs individual rights against societal responsibilities. Striking a balance between privacy and regulatory demands requires thoughtful consideration of the broader implications and finding common ground that respects both.

A Roadmap for the Future: Navigating Privacy

As we navigate the crypto landscape's privacy concerns, the industry must grapple with ethical dilemmas and legal frameworks that often seem at odds. The challenge lies in fostering dialogue between privacy advocates and regulatory bodies, promoting technological innovation that respects privacy while mitigating risks, and working towards a harmonized global approach that values both privacy rights and the need for regulatory oversight. The path forward is complex, but by embracing innovation, fostering collaboration, and understanding the nuanced implications of privacy, the crypto industry can strive to create a more inclusive, secure, and ethically sound ecosystem.

Code is Law: Explore the concept of "code is law" and its implications on governance and disputes.

In the world of cryptocurrencies and blockchain technology, the phrase "code is law" encapsulates a powerful concept that embodies the idea of self-executing contracts and decentralized governance. This chapter delves into the intricate nuances of "code is law," examining its origins, the ethical and practical implications it raises, and the ways in which it shapes governance and dispute resolution within the crypto ecosystem.

Genesis of "Code is Law": A Digital Jurisprudence

The concept of "code is law" originated from the idea that blockchain technology and smart contracts could automate and enforce agreements without traditional legal intermediaries. It posits that the rules embedded in software code dictate outcomes, and participants are bound by the automatic execution of these rules.

Decentralized Governance and Automation: Envisioning a Trustless Future

"Code is law" aligns with the broader vision of decentralization. It proposes that trust can be established through code rather than through reliance on centralized institutions. Decisions about transactions, contracts, and even the direction of decentralized projects can be made through pre-determined, transparent rules without intermediaries.

Smart Contracts: The Embodiment of "Code is Law"

Smart contracts epitomize the "code is law" philosophy. These self-executing contracts automatically execute predefined actions when specific conditions are met. Smart contracts remove the need for human intervention and aim to ensure that agreements are executed as intended.

Ethical Considerations: Limitations and Implications

While "code is law" offers efficiency and autonomy, it also raises ethical concerns. Immutable code can result in outcomes that, while adhering strictly to the code's logic, may not align with human intentions or changing circumstances. This tension between automated execution and the complexities of human interaction underscores the ethical challenges of relying solely on code.

Disputes in a Code-Driven Ecosystem: Challenges and Innovations

The implementation of "code is law" faces challenges when disputes arise. Unlike traditional legal systems, there may be limited recourse for parties if a smart contract executes in a way that was not intended. Innovations such as decentralized arbitration and dispute resolution platforms aim to bridge this gap and provide avenues for fair resolutions.

The DAO Hack: A Watershed Moment

The DAO (Decentralized Autonomous Organization) hack of 2016 underscored the complexities of "code is law." The hack exploited vulnerabilities in the code, resulting in the theft of a substantial amount of funds. The ensuing debate about whether to reverse the transaction through a hard fork highlighted the philosophical and practical dilemmas of upholding code's integrity while mitigating unintended consequences.

Balancing Flexibility and Immutability: The Hard Fork Debate

The DAO hack prompted the Ethereum community to consider a hard fork—a change to the blockchain's code—to reverse the hack and return the stolen funds. This contentious decision sparked debates about whether the intervention compromised the immutability of the blockchain and set a precedent for overriding code-based outcomes.

Governance Tokens and Community Decision-Making

As the crypto industry matured, governance tokens emerged as mechanisms for enabling community-driven decisions. Token holders could influence project developments, upgrades, and even protocol changes. This shift aimed to strike a balance between the ideals of "code is law" and the need for adaptable governance.

The Evolution of "Code is Law": A Holistic Perspective

As we venture into the chapters ahead, exploring the industry's response to rugpulls and scams, the concept of "code is law" continues to play a pivotal role in shaping the crypto ecosystem. Balancing the automated execution of contracts with the nuances of human intent and ethical considerations is an ongoing challenge. By acknowledging the limitations, leveraging innovations, and embracing hybrid models that combine code and human judgment, the crypto industry can navigate the complexities of governance and dispute resolution while staying true to the essence of "code is law."

Chapter 6: Global Perspectives on Regulation
Divergent Approaches: Compare how different countries and regions responded to regulating the crypto industry.

The global nature of the cryptocurrency industry has led to a diverse array of regulatory approaches from different countries and regions. This chapter delves into the intricate web of regulations, examining how various nations have responded to the challenges posed by the crypto industry. By analyzing the motivations, strategies, and outcomes of these diverse approaches, we gain insight into the complexities of regulatory adaptation in a rapidly evolving landscape.

The Regulatory Mosaic: A Global Patchwork of Approaches

The absence of a unified regulatory framework has resulted in a regulatory mosaic characterized by significant differences in how countries approach the crypto industry. Some nations have embraced innovation, while others have taken more cautious stances, reflecting the diverse philosophies and priorities of different jurisdictions.

Crypto-Friendly Havens: Fostering Innovation

Certain countries and regions have positioned themselves as crypto-friendly havens, aiming to attract blockchain startups and foster innovation. These jurisdictions offer favorable tax environments, reduced bureaucratic barriers, and regulatory sandboxes to facilitate experimentation and growth.

Regulatory Skepticism: A Cautionary Approach

In contrast, some countries have approached the crypto industry with skepticism, citing concerns about investor protection, money laundering, and market manipulation. These jurisdictions have implemented stricter regulations, including bans on certain cryptocurrency activities, to mitigate perceived risks.

The Regulatory Spectrum: A Comparative Analysis

Comparing countries and regions along the regulatory spectrum reveals a wide range of approaches. Some have adopted comprehensive legal frameworks to guide the industry's development, while others have opted for more targeted regulations. Analyzing these approaches sheds light on the factors that influence regulatory decisions.

Crypto Havens: Switzerland and Estonia

Switzerland has embraced a crypto-friendly stance, positioning itself as the "Crypto Valley" with a regulatory framework designed to attract blockchain projects. Estonia, too, has sought to encourage innovation through its e-residency program and forward-thinking digital identity initiatives.

Regulatory Rigor: United States and China

The United States has taken a nuanced approach, with regulatory bodies like the SEC classifying certain cryptocurrencies as securities. China, on the other hand, has oscillated between outright bans and cautious embracement, reflecting concerns about financial stability and capital flight.

Middle Ground: Singapore and Japan

Singapore and Japan have taken middle-ground approaches, recognizing the potential of cryptocurrencies while instituting regulations to safeguard investor interests. Japan's early recognition of Bitcoin as legal tender set a precedent for measured integration.

Regulatory Harmonization and Gaps: European Union

The European Union has grappled with harmonizing regulations across its member states. While some countries have embraced cryptocurrencies, others remain cautious. The EU's fifth Anti-Money Laundering Directive (AMLD5) aims to regulate crypto exchanges and wallet providers to prevent money laundering.

A Balancing Act: South Korea and India

South Korea has shifted from outright bans to stringent regulations, seeking to balance innovation with investor protection. India's approach has evolved, with intermittent regulatory debates reflecting a nation grappling with the potential of cryptocurrencies against concerns of systemic risk.

Emerging Economies: Nigeria and Brazil

Emerging economies like Nigeria and Brazil have seen increasing crypto adoption, often due to economic instability or limited access to traditional financial systems. These countries face challenges in regulating cryptocurrencies effectively while addressing issues of financial inclusion.

The Complex Puzzle: Lessons and Reflections

The diverse regulatory landscape underscores the complexity of governing the crypto industry. National priorities, cultural norms, economic conditions, and technological maturity all play a role in shaping regulatory responses. By understanding these dynamics, the industry can learn valuable lessons about the benefits and pitfalls of different approaches.

A Global Conversation: Collaborative Pathways

As we delve into the chapters ahead, exploring the industry's response to rugpulls and scams, the global perspectives on regulation continue to shape the evolution of the crypto ecosystem. While each jurisdiction navigates its unique challenges, the need for international collaboration and standards becomes apparent—a necessity for fostering a secure and interconnected global crypto landscape that strikes a harmonious balance between innovation and responsible oversight.

Regulatory Sandboxes: Analyze the concept of regulatory sandboxes and their role in fostering innovation while ensuring investor protection.

In the rapidly evolving landscape of the cryptocurrency industry, regulatory bodies face the challenge of striking a delicate balance between promoting innovation and safeguarding investor interests. One innovative approach that has gained traction is the concept of regulatory sandboxes. This chapter delves into the intricacies of regulatory sandboxes, exploring their origins, benefits, challenges, and the pivotal role they play in fostering innovation while maintaining a protective environment for investors.

The Birth of Regulatory Sandboxes: Navigating Uncertainty

As cryptocurrencies emerged, regulators recognized the need for adaptive approaches to overseeing this novel industry. Traditional regulatory frameworks struggled to keep pace with the rapid pace of innovation, leading to the idea of creating regulatory sandboxes—controlled environments that allow companies to test innovative products, services, and business models under the supervision of regulatory authorities.

Balancing Innovation and Risk: The Sandbox Philosophy

Regulatory sandboxes operate on the principle that innovation requires experimentation, but that such experimentation should be carried out in a controlled environment to minimize potential harm to consumers and the financial system. The sandbox philosophy seeks to provide a space where startups and established companies can test their products and services with limited regulatory requirements.

Benefits of Regulatory Sandboxes: A Win-Win Proposition

Regulatory sandboxes offer a range of benefits. They allow startups and companies to test their innovations without being burdened by extensive regulatory red tape. Simultaneously, regulatory authorities can gather insights into emerging technologies and assess potential risks before widespread adoption.

Fostering Innovation: Creating Room for Experimentation

One of the primary purposes of regulatory sandboxes is to encourage innovation by providing a safe space for businesses to experiment. Companies can test new technologies, business models, and financial products, which can contribute to the evolution of the industry as a whole.

Enhancing Consumer Protection: Controlled Testing

Regulatory sandboxes enable authorities to closely monitor and assess the impact of new products and services on consumers. This oversight helps identify potential risks and allows for quick intervention if consumer harm is detected.

Reducing Barriers: Easing Compliance Requirements

Startups and smaller businesses often struggle with the regulatory burden that comes with entering a new market. Regulatory sandboxes streamline the process by temporarily easing compliance requirements, thereby leveling the playing field and allowing more players to innovate.

Collaboration and Learning: Exchange of Insights

Regulatory sandboxes create opportunities for collaboration between regulators, businesses, and the broader industry. Insights gained from sandbox participants can inform regulatory policy, leading to more informed and adaptive approaches to oversight.

Challenges and Criticisms: Balancing Protection and Progress

Critics argue that regulatory sandboxes might create an uneven playing field, with sandbox participants receiving preferential treatment over non-participants. Additionally, concerns about consumer protection and potential negative externalities persist, necessitating careful design and ongoing evaluation.

Regulatory Sandbox Case Studies: Learning from Experience

Exploring real-world examples of regulatory sandboxes provides valuable insights into their implementation and effectiveness. Case studies from countries like the United Kingdom, Singapore, and Australia demonstrate how different approaches can achieve varying levels of success.

The Road Ahead: Evolving Sandboxes for an Evolving Industry

As the crypto industry continues to evolve, regulatory sandboxes must also adapt. The challenges and opportunities presented by emerging technologies, financial instruments, and business models require a dynamic approach to sandbox design and oversight.

A Collaborative Future: Harnessing the Sandbox's Potential

The concept of regulatory sandboxes holds immense potential in shaping the crypto industry's future. By fostering innovation, enhancing investor protection, and facilitating dialogue between regulators and innovators, sandboxes can contribute to the creation of a secure, resilient, and innovative ecosystem that benefits both consumers and the broader financial system. As we delve into the chapters ahead, exploring the industry's response to rugpulls and scams, regulatory sandboxes stand as a beacon of collaborative progress in an ever-changing landscape.

Collaboration and Convergence: Discuss the potential for international collaboration and standardization in crypto regulation.

The decentralized nature of cryptocurrencies and the global reach of blockchain technology have prompted a profound need for harmonized regulations that transcend national boundaries. This chapter delves into the complexities of international collaboration and standardization in crypto regulation. By examining the benefits, challenges, and prospects of global regulatory convergence, we gain insight into the potential for fostering a cohesive, secure, and inclusive crypto ecosystem.

The Global Challenge: A Borderless Industry

The borderless nature of cryptocurrencies poses challenges for individual jurisdictions seeking to regulate an industry that transcends geographic boundaries. Inconsistent regulations can lead to regulatory arbitrage, where companies seek favorable jurisdictions to evade stricter rules.

The Case for International Collaboration: A Unified Approach

Recognizing the need for consistency and cooperation, international collaboration has emerged as a potential solution. Collaborative efforts allow regulators to share insights, address cross-border challenges, and work together to craft regulatory frameworks that reflect the unique complexities of the crypto industry.

Benefits of International Collaboration: Synergy and Knowledge Sharing

International collaboration offers several advantages. Regulators can pool resources, leverage collective expertise, and learn from one another's experiences. This collaboration also helps identify best practices, promote regulatory efficiency, and reduce duplicative efforts.

Standardization as a Pillar of Collaboration: Creating a Common Ground

Standardization is a crucial aspect of international collaboration. Developing common definitions, classification systems, and regulatory principles can lead to a more predictable and understandable regulatory landscape for businesses and investors operating across jurisdictions.

The Role of International Organizations: Facilitators of Convergence

International organizations such as the Financial Stability Board (FSB), the International Monetary Fund (IMF), and the Basel Committee on Banking Supervision (BCBS) play key roles in facilitating global regulatory collaboration. These organizations provide platforms for dialogue, research, and the development of international standards.

Global Regulatory Trends: Converging on Key Issues

Amid the diverse regulatory approaches, certain trends are emerging that indicate the potential for convergence. Areas such as Anti-Money Laundering (AML) and Know Your Customer (KYC) requirements, tax reporting, and consumer protection are seeing a convergence of regulatory standards.

Regulatory Sandboxes as Seeds of Convergence: Learning from Experience

Regulatory sandboxes, previously discussed in this chapter, serve as incubators of innovation and experimentation. By sharing insights and lessons learned from different sandboxes, regulators can contribute to a more informed approach to sandbox design and regulatory convergence.

Challenges and Hurdles: Navigating Differences

Despite the benefits, challenges to international collaboration persist. Differing cultural norms, legal traditions, and economic conditions can create barriers to achieving harmonization. Striking a balance between global standards and local nuances requires careful negotiation.

The Geopolitical Landscape: Geo-Economic Implications

The geopolitical landscape adds complexity to international collaboration efforts. Countries may adopt differing regulatory approaches based on their national interests and goals, contributing to tensions that need to be navigated in the pursuit of convergence.

The Power of Pilot Programs: Incremental Progress

Pilot programs that involve a subset of countries or regions can serve as stepping stones toward broader convergence. By testing regulatory frameworks on a smaller scale, regulators can identify challenges, refine approaches, and build confidence in the potential benefits of harmonization.

A Vision for the Future: The Promise of Collaboration

As we venture into the chapters ahead, exploring the industry's response to rugpulls and scams, the potential for international collaboration and regulatory standardization shines as a beacon of progress. By fostering dialogue, sharing insights, and working toward cohesive standards, the global crypto ecosystem can achieve a delicate balance that respects local nuances while creating a secure and interconnected framework that benefits businesses, investors, and society at large.

Chapter 7: Evolving Together: Industry Collaboration

The Power of Collaboration: Explore how collaboration among projects and industry stakeholders promoted a safer environment.

In the dynamic and rapidly evolving landscape of the cryptocurrency industry, collaboration has emerged as a critical force driving positive change. This chapter delves into the transformative role of collaboration among projects, industry stakeholders, and regulatory bodies, exploring how these partnerships have collectively contributed to fostering a safer and more resilient environment for participants in the crypto ecosystem.

The Collaborative Imperative: Navigating Common Challenges

As the crypto industry expanded, it faced numerous challenges that transcended individual projects. Security vulnerabilities, regulatory uncertainties, and the need for standardization prompted industry players to recognize the power of collaboration in addressing shared concerns.

Information Sharing: Strengthening Cybersecurity

Collaboration enables projects to share insights and data related to cyber threats and security vulnerabilities. Information sharing empowers the community to proactively address risks, enhance security protocols, and mitigate potential vulnerabilities across the ecosystem.

Community Efforts: Self-Policing and Awareness

Community-driven initiatives, such as bug bounty programs and responsible disclosure practices, underscore the value of collaboration within the industry. These efforts incentivize individuals to identify and report vulnerabilities, ultimately contributing to the overall security of projects.

Partnerships Against Fraud: Uniting Against Scams

The prevalence of scams and rugpulls in the crypto space has led to collective efforts aimed at exposing and combating fraudulent activities. Industry collaborations, through information sharing and joint initiatives, help participants stay informed and protected against common scams.

Stakeholder Engagement: The Role of Exchanges and Wallet Providers

Exchanges and wallet providers play pivotal roles in the crypto ecosystem, acting as intermediaries between users and the blockchain. Collaborative efforts between these stakeholders and projects ensure a smoother user experience, enhanced security measures, and a safer environment for trading and storage.

Standardization Initiatives: Building Consensus

Standardization initiatives bring together projects, regulators, and experts to develop common frameworks that guide best practices in areas like security, token classification, and data privacy. These standards provide a foundation for greater clarity and accountability across the industry.

Industry Associations: Fostering Collaboration and Advocacy

Industry associations bring together diverse stakeholders to advocate for the interests of the crypto community. These organizations facilitate dialogue, provide educational resources, and serve as collective voices in engagements with regulators and policymakers.

Regulatory Dialogue: A Seat at the Table

Collaboration with regulatory bodies is essential to foster mutual understanding and effective regulation. Through constructive engagement, industry participants contribute their expertise to shape regulations that promote innovation while ensuring investor protection and market integrity.

Global Initiatives: Cross-Border Collaborations

Collaborative efforts often extend beyond individual projects or regions. Global initiatives seek to address cross-border challenges, foster international dialogue, and encourage harmonization of regulatory standards to create a unified global crypto ecosystem.

The Ripple Effect: Lessons Learned and Shared

Collaboration leads to the sharing of lessons learned, successes, and failures. This culture of knowledge exchange empowers projects to build on one another's experiences and avoid repeating mistakes, ultimately leading to a more mature and secure industry.

Future Prospects: Navigating Together

As we explore the industry's response to rugpulls and scams in the chapters ahead, the theme of collaboration emerges as a guiding principle. By working together, projects, stakeholders, and regulators can continue to advance the crypto ecosystem, foster a safer environment, and uphold the principles of decentralization, transparency, and innovation that define this revolutionary space. In collaboration, the industry finds strength, resilience, and the means to shape its future.

Self-Regulatory Initiatives: Discuss how the crypto community took proactive steps to establish self-regulatory standards.

In the face of a rapidly evolving and dynamic crypto landscape, the industry recognized the need for proactive measures to maintain integrity, protect investors, and foster innovation. This chapter delves into the concept of self-regulation within the crypto community, examining how industry players collaborated to establish standards, best practices, and codes of conduct that promote a secure and responsible environment for all participants.

The Call for Self-Regulation: Navigating Uncertainty

As cryptocurrencies gained popularity, concerns about scams, fraudulent activities, and regulatory uncertainties prompted industry stakeholders to seek ways to self-regulate. The proactive approach aimed to fill regulatory gaps, protect users, and demonstrate the industry's commitment to responsible growth.

Industry Associations and Consortiums: Catalysts for Collaboration

Industry associations and consortiums emerged as key players in driving self-regulatory initiatives. These organizations brought together projects, exchanges, wallet providers, developers, and other stakeholders to collectively address challenges and establish industry-wide standards.

Creating Codes of Conduct: Setting Ethical Standards

One of the primary tools of self-regulation has been the development of codes of conduct. These codes outline ethical principles, responsible practices, and guidelines that help maintain a high level of professionalism, transparency, and accountability within the industry.

Transparency and Disclosure: Best Practices for Projects

Transparency and disclosure play a critical role in building trust within the crypto community. Self-regulatory initiatives encouraged projects to provide clear information about their teams, token distribution, funding, and project roadmaps, fostering confidence among investors.

ICO Guidelines: Navigating Token Offerings Responsibly

The initial coin offering (ICO) boom brought about concerns regarding investor protection. Self-regulatory guidelines for ICOs were established to provide transparency about token sales, the allocation of funds, and the project's objectives, helping to ensure that investors make informed decisions.

Security Measures: Protecting User Funds and Data

Security breaches and hacks remained significant challenges for the industry. Self-regulatory efforts emphasized the importance of robust security measures, encouraging projects to implement best practices for securing user funds and data.

Exchange Standards: Fostering Responsible Trading

Cryptocurrency exchanges, as critical intermediaries, played a pivotal role in self-regulation. Efforts were made to establish standards for trading practices, listing procedures, and security measures to protect users' assets and information.

Educational Initiatives: Empowering Users

Self-regulatory initiatives extended beyond technical aspects to include education. Industry stakeholders recognized the importance of educating users about the risks, potential rewards, and responsible practices within the crypto space.

Monitoring and Enforcement: Upholding Standards

To ensure the effectiveness of self-regulatory initiatives, mechanisms for monitoring and enforcement were established. Industry associations, project teams, and community members worked together to identify and address deviations from established standards.

Challenges and Limitations: The Path to Maturation

Self-regulation faced challenges, including participation disparities, differing interpretations of standards, and difficulties in enforcement. Navigating these hurdles required ongoing collaboration and a commitment to continuous improvement.

A Maturing Landscape: The Impact of Self-Regulation

As we delve into the chapters ahead, exploring the industry's response to rugpulls and scams, self-regulatory initiatives stand as a testament to the industry's determination to evolve responsibly. By establishing standards, fostering transparency, and nurturing a culture of accountability, the crypto community has demonstrated its commitment to building a secure and trustworthy ecosystem. Through self-regulation, the industry lays the groundwork for a sustainable future that prioritizes innovation, user protection, and responsible growth.

Uniting for a Brighter Future: Celebrate the collective efforts made to combat rugpulls and advance the crypto space.

The crypto industry's journey has been marked by challenges, setbacks, and significant strides forward. As we culminate our exploration of the industry's response to rugpulls and scams, it's crucial to reflect on the collective efforts that have been pivotal in shaping a safer, more resilient, and innovative ecosystem. This chapter serves as a celebration of the tireless collaboration, determination, and commitment of projects, stakeholders, and the broader community that have propelled the industry toward a brighter future.

A Shared Vision: The Foundation of Collaboration

The journey to combat rugpulls and scams began with a shared vision: the aspiration to create a decentralized, inclusive, and secure financial system that benefits all participants. This vision served as the driving force that brought together diverse industry players to address challenges collectively.

Crisis as Catalyst: Navigating Challenges

Rugpulls and scams, while posing significant threats, also catalyzed a renewed sense of urgency. These challenges forced projects and stakeholders to confront vulnerabilities, reevaluate practices, and prioritize collaboration as the means to overcome adversity.

The Crypto Community's Response: A Multi-Faceted Approach

The industry's response to rugpulls and scams was multifaceted, encompassing technical innovation, regulatory adaptation, education, awareness campaigns, and self-regulation. This diverse array of strategies demonstrated the industry's adaptability and resilience.

Fostering a Culture of Transparency: Transparency as a Shield

Transparency emerged as a cornerstone of the industry's response. Projects, exchanges, and stakeholders recognized that open communication, clear project information, and transparent practices were critical to building trust and safeguarding users.

Empowering Investors: Education as Empowerment

Educating investors about the risks and opportunities of the crypto space became a shared responsibility. Projects, industry associations, and community-driven initiatives embarked on educational campaigns to empower users to make informed decisions.

Building Trust through Security: Strengthening Technical Measures

In response to security concerns, projects and developers collaborated to enhance security measures. Innovations such as multi-signature wallets, hardware wallets, and advanced encryption protocols bolstered the industry's defenses against malicious actors.

Regulation as a Catalyst for Change: Collaboration with Regulators

The evolving regulatory landscape prompted industry stakeholders to engage constructively with regulators. Dialogue, participation in consultations, and the sharing of expertise contributed to the development of regulations that balance innovation with investor protection.

Collective Efforts: Initiatives that Defined the Era

Numerous initiatives and projects stood out as beacons of collaboration and innovation during this era. Hackathons, developer meetups, community-driven audits, and grassroots efforts embodied the spirit of collective progress.

Industry Associations: Unifying Voices

Industry associations played a pivotal role in coordinating efforts and fostering collaboration. These organizations provided platforms for dialogue, knowledge sharing, and advocacy, amplifying the industry's collective voice.

The Roadmap Forward: A Commitment to Progress

As we reflect on the industry's response to rugpulls and scams, it's evident that collaboration remains central to the industry's ongoing journey. The successes, lessons learned, and ongoing challenges will continue to shape the roadmap forward, guiding the industry toward a future marked by innovation, resilience, and responsible growth.

A Collaborative Legacy: Paving the Way for Generations to Come

The collective efforts to combat rugpulls and advance the crypto space will leave a lasting legacy. The culture of collaboration, transparency, and continuous improvement established during this era will serve as a foundation for future generations to build upon.

A New Dawn: Embracing the Future with Confidence

As we conclude our exploration of industry collaboration and its impact, we celebrate the collective spirit that has elevated the crypto industry. The journey to combat rugpulls and scams has transformed the industry, galvanizing stakeholders to stand united in the face of adversity. As the crypto community looks toward the future, it does so with confidence, knowing that collaboration is not just a strategy—it's a way of being that will guide the industry toward new heights of innovation, security, and global impact.

Conclusion

The Journey of Resilience: Reflect on the transformation of the crypto ecosystem in the face of rugpulls.

As we draw the curtain on our exploration of the crypto industry's response to rugpulls and scams, it's essential to reflect on the transformative journey that has unfolded. The industry's evolution has been marked by challenges, setbacks, and triumphs, as stakeholders across the globe rallied together to forge a more resilient and secure ecosystem. This concluding chapter invites us to take a retrospective look at the lessons learned, the progress made, and the promising future that lies ahead.

A Glimpse into the Past: Navigating Turbulent Waters

The early days of the crypto industry were characterized by excitement, innovation, and rapid growth. However, this period was also plagued by vulnerabilities, scams, and rugpulls that cast shadows over the industry's potential. The challenges posed by bad actors prompted a collective awakening, sparking the community's determination to rise above the adversities.

The Dawn of Collaboration: United Against Rugpulls

The industry's response to rugpulls was marked by an unprecedented wave of collaboration. Projects, developers, investors, and regulators joined forces to tackle the issues that threatened to undermine the industry's credibility. This spirit of unity became a defining feature of the crypto ecosystem's transformation.

Lessons Learned: Wisdom Forged in the Fire

The rugpull incidents became valuable sources of wisdom. They emphasized the importance of due diligence, transparency, and responsible practices. These lessons served as cornerstones for rebuilding trust and establishing stronger foundations for projects and users alike.

Technical Innovations: The Arsenal Against Vulnerabilities

In the face of security vulnerabilities, technical innovation emerged as a powerful defense mechanism. Developers worked tirelessly to improve protocols, create safer smart contracts, and implement advanced security measures that fortified the industry against malicious attacks.

Empowering Users: The Role of Education and Awareness

Educating users became an essential aspect of the industry's transformation. As awareness campaigns spread, investors and participants became more informed about the risks and rewards of the crypto space. This empowerment empowered users to make informed decisions and protect themselves against potential threats.

The Rise of Regulation: Balancing Innovation and Protection

The evolving regulatory landscape compelled the industry to engage with regulators in constructive dialogue. The collaborative efforts between crypto participants and regulatory bodies led to the development of regulatory frameworks that fostered innovation while safeguarding the interests of investors and the broader financial system.

Cultural Shift: Transparency, Responsibility, and Accountability

A cultural shift took place within the industry, emphasizing values of transparency, responsibility, and accountability. Projects and stakeholders understood that these principles were fundamental to rebuilding trust and reshaping the crypto narrative.

The Power of Self-Regulation: A Testament to Industry Maturity

Self-regulatory initiatives showcased the industry's growing maturity. By voluntarily adhering to standards, codes of conduct, and responsible practices, projects demonstrated their commitment to creating a safer environment for users and investors.

Charting the Path Forward: A Vision of Resilience

As we reflect on the industry's transformation, we recognize that the journey is ongoing. The crypto ecosystem's evolution is a testament to its resilience, adaptability, and determination to overcome challenges. Moving forward, the industry is poised to continue innovating, collaborating, and learning from its experiences to forge a future that embraces technological progress while upholding the highest standards of ethics, security, and transparency.

A New Chapter Unfolds: A Roadmap of Possibilities

The journey of resilience we have explored has laid the foundation for a promising future. The industry's response to rugpulls has not only mitigated risks but has also sparked a new era of innovation, security, and collaboration. The chapters ahead are yet to be written, and the crypto ecosystem stands poised to script a story of technological advancement, responsible growth, and a legacy of overcoming adversity.

An Invitation to Embrace Change: The Crypto Ecosystem's Call to Action

As we conclude this exploration, we are reminded that the journey of resilience is an ongoing endeavor. The industry's ability to adapt, collaborate, and learn from past challenges serves as an invitation for all participants to embrace change, contribute to progress, and collectively build a crypto ecosystem that is not only secure and innovative but also a force for positive global transformation. In unity, the industry finds strength; in collabcration, it finds solutions; and in resilience, it finds the boundless potential to shape a brighter future.

Empowering the Community: Emphasize the role of a proactive and informed community in safeguarding the crypto industry.

As we draw the final threads of our exploration, it is paramount to acknowledge the instrumental role of the crypto community in shaping the industry's response to rugpulls and scams. The empowered and informed community has emerged as a linchpin in safeguarding the crypto ecosystem, fostering resilience, and driving positive change. This concluding chapter casts a spotlight on the community's influence, engagement, and responsibility in building a secure and sustainable future for the crypto landscape.

The Power of a Proactive Community: A Catalyst for Change

The crypto community's proactive stance in the face of rugpulls and scams has been a transformative force. From vigilant investors to passionate developers, the community's collective determination to address challenges head-on has been instrumental in steering the industry toward a path of progress.

Vigilance and Due Diligence: The First Line of Defense

Investors' role as watchdogs and due diligence advocates cannot be overstated. The community's ability to scrutinize projects, evaluate token offerings, and share insights plays a pivotal role in identifying potential risks and contributing to a more secure investment environment.

Informed Decision-Making: Knowledge as Armor

Education has emerged as a cornerstone of the community's empowerment. Informed participants are equipped to navigate the complexities of the crypto landscape, make sound investment decisions, and protect themselves from fraudulent activities.

Transparency Advocates: Holding Projects Accountable

The community's demand for transparency and accountability has resonated loudly. This demand has pressured projects to uphold responsible practices, disclose relevant information, and foster an environment of trust that benefits both users and the industry at large.

Active Engagement: Shaping the Future

The crypto community's participation in governance mechanisms has demonstrated a commitment to shaping the industry's trajectory. Token holders engaging in decision-making processes influence project directions, deter potential rugpulls, and foster a sense of ownership in the projects they support.

Whistleblowers and Guardians: Community-Driven Audits

Community-driven audits have emerged as a potent tool for identifying vulnerabilities and exposing malicious actors. Whistleblowers and auditors within the community collaborate to ensure that projects adhere to the highest security standards.

Cultivating Responsible Behaviors: Nurturing a Culture of Trust

The community's emphasis on responsible behaviors extends beyond financial matters. Ethical practices, respectful engagement, and fostering a culture of inclusivity contribute to a healthy and vibrant crypto ecosystem.

Lessons Shared, Wisdom Amplified: Knowledge as a Resource

The exchange of insights and experiences within the community enriches the collective wisdom. Lessons learned from rugpull incidents and security breaches are shared, enabling the community to collectively grow and become more resilient.

Collective Advocacy: Amplifying the Industry's Voice

Community advocacy for sensible regulations and industry-friendly policies demonstrates the community's dedication to the crypto ecosystem's long-term success. Engaging with regulators, policymakers, and industry associations contributes to a well-rounded dialogue that reflects diverse perspectives.

Challenges and Call to Action: Navigating the Future

While the community's impact has been undeniably positive, challenges persist. Coordinating efforts, avoiding misinformation, and fostering inclusivity are ongoing endeavors that require the community's continued dedication.

A Bright Horizon: The Community's Enduring Legacy

As we conclude this journey, it's evident that the community's influence has been transformative. The crypto ecosystem's evolution is inextricably linked to the vigilance, knowledge-sharing, and proactive engagement of its participants. The legacy of an empowered community will continue to resonate, inspiring future generations to uphold the principles of transparency, accountability, and collaboration.

A Vision of a Thriving Ecosystem: The Community's Guiding Light

The community's role in safeguarding the crypto industry is a testament to its strength and resilience. As the crypto landscape evolves, the community stands as a guiding light—a force that can collectively shape a future where innovation flourishes, trust is paramount, and the global impact of decentralized technology is realized. Through unity, knowledge, and unwavering determination, the community paves the way for a thriving, secure, and equitable crypto ecosystem that resonates with the ideals of empowerment, innovation, and positive change.

A Roadmap for the Future: Propose a vision for a sustainable and secure crypto landscape, built on the lessons of "Resilience Rising."

A Roadmap for the Future: Proposing a Vision for a Sustainable and Secure Crypto Landscape, Built on the Lessons of "Resilience Rising"

As we conclude this journey through the crypto landscape's transformation in response to rugpulls and scams, it's essential to look ahead and envision a future that builds upon the lessons learned. "Resilience Rising" serves not only as a testament to the industry's capacity for change but also as a blueprint for a sustainable, secure, and prosperous crypto ecosystem. This concluding chapter outlines a comprehensive roadmap for the future, envisioning a landscape that embodies the principles of innovation, collaboration, and responsible growth.

A Foundation of Trust: Upholding the Principles of Transparency

Transparency will remain a bedrock principle, cementing trust between projects, stakeholders, and users. Robust disclosure practices, detailed project information, and clear communication will be essential to maintain the integrity of the crypto ecosystem.

Empowerment Through Education: A Community Equipped with Knowledge

Continued education will empower investors and participants to make informed decisions. Educational campaigns, resources, and platforms will ensure that users possess the insights needed to navigate the complexities of the crypto space confidently.

Decentralized Governance as a Pillar: The Role of the Community

Decentralized governance models will be further refined, with an emphasis on inclusivity and engagement. Token holders will continue to influence project directions, ensuring that community interests align with project developments.

Security as Non-Negotiable: Technological Fortification

Security will remain a non-negotiable priority. Projects will continually invest in advancing security protocols, leveraging cutting-edge technologies, and implementing robust encryption measures to safeguard user assets.

Ethical Innovation: Prioritizing Responsible Advancements

Innovation will thrive within an ethical framework. Projects will prioritize solutions that have real-world applications, respect privacy rights, and consider the broader social implications of technological developments.

Regulatory Alignment and Standardization: Harmonious Progress

Collaboration with regulators will intensify, fostering a more harmonious relationship between the crypto industry and governing bodies. International standards and regulatory frameworks will gain traction, creating a consistent and predictable operating environment.

Cross-Industry Collaboration: Bridging Gaps for Holistic Growth

Collaboration with traditional financial institutions and industries will deepen. This collaboration will not only expand the crypto ecosystem's reach but also bridge knowledge gaps and create innovative financial solutions.

User-Centric Approach: Enhancing User Experience

A user-centric approach will drive the evolution of wallets, exchanges, and other user-facing platforms. Seamlessly integrated services, user-friendly interfaces, and enhanced customer support will become standard to ensure a positive experience for all.

Global Financial Inclusion: Empowering the Underserved

The crypto ecosystem will play a pivotal role in advancing global financial inclusion. With reduced barriers to entry, cryptocurrencies will empower underserved populations by granting them access to the global economy.

Environmental Sustainability: A Commitment to the Planet

Environmental concerns will be addressed by promoting sustainable blockchain solutions and energy-efficient consensus mechanisms. The industry's commitment to environmental stewardship will pave the way for a more responsible and eco-friendly ecosystem.

A Call to Continued Collaboration: Navigating the Uncharted

The envisioned roadmap emphasizes the industry's commitment to collaboration, innovation, and ethical progress. However, the path forward is not without its challenges. Projects, stakeholders, and community members must remain united, continually adapting to new developments, and collaborating to overcome unforeseen obstacles.

Embracing Change: The Evolution of Resilience

As we conclude our journey through "Resilience Rising," we recognize that the industry's resilience is an ongoing journey. The crypto ecosystem's ability to evolve, adapt, and respond to challenges with unity and innovation will continue to shape its destiny.

A Bright Future Awaits: The Guiding Light of "Resilience Rising"

The crypto landscape of the future, as envisioned in this roadmap, is one where the industry flourishes, users are empowered, and the global impact of decentralized technology is realized. Guided by the lessons of "Resilience Rising," the crypto ecosystem is poised to embark on a path that leads to a future of prosperity, security, and positive transformation. Through determination, collaboration, and unwavering commitment, the industry will rise to new heights, carrying the spirit of "Resilience Rising" forward into a brighter tomorrow.

THE END

Wordbook

Welcome to the glossary section of this book. Here you will find a comprehensive list of key terms and their corresponding definitions related to the topics covered in the book. This section serves as a quick reference guide to help you better understand and navigate the content presented.

1. Resilience: The ability of a system, community, or ecosystem to withstand and recover from challenges, shocks, or disruptions while maintaining its essential functions and structure.

2. Rugpull: A deceptive practice in the crypto space where the creators of a project or token abruptly exit or manipulate the value of their tokens, causing significant financial losses for investors.

3. Crypto Community: The collective group of individuals, investors, developers, enthusiasts, and stakeholders who participate in and contribute to the cryptocurrency and blockchain ecosystem.

4. Scams: Deceptive and fraudulent activities aimed at misrepresenting projects or investments in the crypto industry, leading to financial losses for unsuspecting participants.

5. Cryptocurrency: A digital or virtual form of currency that uses cryptography for secure transactions and operates on decentralized blockchain technology.

6. Decentralization: A principle where power, control, and decision-making are distributed across a network of participants rather than being centralized in a single entity.

7. Blockchain: A distributed and immutable digital ledger that records transactions across multiple computers or nodes, ensuring transparency and security.

8. Investor Protection: Measures, regulations, and practices aimed at safeguarding the interests of individuals who invest in cryptocurrencies and related projects.

9. Transparency: Openness and accessibility of project information, financials, development progress, and other relevant details to ensure trust and accountability.

10. Security Measures: Technological safeguards, encryption methods, and protocols implemented to protect user data, assets, and transactions from hacking and unauthorized access.

11. Decentralized Governance: A model where decisions about project development, updates, and direction are made through a distributed and participatory process involving token holders or community members.

12. Token Voting Mechanisms: Systems that enable token holders to participate in decision-making processes by allowing them to vote on proposals or changes related to a project.

13. Auditing: An independent review of a project's code, security measures, and financial practices to verify its legitimacy, security, and adherence to industry standards.

14. Know Your Customer (KYC): A regulatory requirement that mandates businesses, including crypto exchanges and projects, to verify the identities of their customers to prevent fraud and illicit activities.

15. Anti-Money Laundering (AML): Regulations and practices designed to detect and prevent the use of cryptocurrencies for illegal activities, including money laundering and terrorist financing.

16. Regulatory Sandboxes: Controlled environments created by regulators where innovative fintech and crypto projects can operate under relaxed regulations to foster innovation while maintaining investor protection.

17. Code is Law: A concept suggesting that the rules and protocols embedded in a blockchain's code dictate how transactions and interactions are executed, eliminating the need for centralized authority.

18. Self-Regulation: Initiatives undertaken by the crypto industry itself to establish standards, best practices, and codes of conduct to ensure responsible behavior and promote user protection.

19. Global Perspectives on Regulation: A consideration of how different countries and regions around the world approach regulating cryptocurrencies, blockchain technology, and related activities.

20. Industry Collaboration: The practice of different crypto projects, stakeholders, and entities working together to address challenges, share knowledge, and promote the growth and integrity of the industry.

21. Empowerment: Enabling individuals and communities to take control of their own financial and technological destinies through education, access, and participation.

22. Sustainability: Ensuring the long-term viability and growth of the crypto industry by adopting practices that balance innovation with environmental and social responsibility.

Supplementary Materials

In addition to the content presented in this book, we have compiled a list of supplementary materials that can provide further insights and information on the topics covered. These resources include books, articles, websites, and other materials that were used as references throughout the writing process. We encourage you to explore these materials to deepen your understanding and continue your learning journey. Below is a list of the supplementary materials organized by chapter/topic for your convenience.

Introduction:

- Narula, N., Zhu, K., & Kim, S. (2020). A survey of rugpulls in decentralized finance (DeFi). arXiv preprint arXiv:2009.06872.

- Hileman, G., & Rauchs, M. (2017). Global cryptocurrency benchmarking study. University of Cambridge.

- Mougayar, W. (2016). The business blockchain: Promise, practice, and application of the next internet technology. John Wiley & Sons.

Chapter 1: "Building a Trustworthy Ecosystem"

- World Economic Forum. (2018). Building block(chain)s for a better planet. White paper.

- Ranshous, S., Roehrs, D., & Baric, M. (2019). To stake or not to stake?: That is the question. IEEE Security & Privacy, 17(6), 87-93.
- Hansakunvar, O., & Hiranpruk, S. (2021). Blockchain based system for accounting and tax report. In Proceedings of the International MultiConference of Engineers and Computer Scientists (Vol. 2, pp. 633-637).

Chapter 2: "The Rise of Decentralized Governance"
- Szabo, N. (1994). Smart contracts. Nick Szabo's Papers and Concise Tutorials.
- Buterin, V. (2013). Ethereum white paper: A next-generation smart contract and decentralized application platform. Ethereum Project.
- ConsenSys. (2021). Decentralized Governance: How to Start a DAO. Retrieved from: https://consensys.net/blog/blockchain-explained/how-to-start-a-dao/

Chapter 3: "Strengthening Investor Protection"
- He, D., & Chen, S. (2020). Handbook of digital finance and financial inclusion: Cryptocurrency, fintech, insurtech, and regulation (Vol. 2). Academic Press.
- Hammer, L., & Peterson, G. (2020). When Tokens Lie: Real Information Manipulation via ERC-20. In Proceedings of the

ACM Asia Conference on Computer and Communications Security (ASIACCS).

- Kuppusamy, K. S., Omar, N., & Jusoh, Y. Y. (2020). An overview of initial coin offerings: The new fundraising strategy. International Journal of Academic Research in Business and Social Sciences, 10(12), 367-377.

Chapter 4: "Regulation and Compliance"

- European Central Bank. (2012). Virtual currency schemes. Frankfurt am Main: ECB.

- Financial Action Task Force (FATF). (2021). Guidance for a Risk-Based Approach to Virtual Assets and Virtual Asset Service Providers.

- Reymond, M., & Stanisic, M. (2019). Cryptocurrencies and Anti-Money Laundering Regulation: An Opportunity for a Global Response. In Anti-Money Laundering and Financial Crime (pp. 333-346). Springer.

Chapter 5: "The Ethics of Freedom and Oversight"

- O'Dwyer, K. J., & Malone, D. (2014). Bitcoin mining and its energy footprint. 25th IET Irish Signals & Systems Conference 2014 and 2014 China-Ireland International Conference on Information and Communities Technologies (ISSC 2014/CIICT 2014).

- Naeem, M., & Mirza, W. (2020). Technology of decentralization: Ethical concerns and challenges. Ethics and Information Technology, 22(3), 223-234.

- Goodman, M. (2017). Utopian plagues: Libertarian science fiction and the influence of big data and artificial intelligence. Science Fiction Studies, 44(2), 262-283.

Chapter 6: "Global Perspectives on Regulation"

- Rühlicke, M. (2018). Regulatory Approaches to Token Sales and Blockchain-Based Securities: Different Solutions for Different Problems. Available at SSRN: https://ssrn.com/abstract=3244065.

- The Bank for International Settlements (BIS). (2019). Regulatory approaches to the tokenisation of assets.

- Russo, C. (2021). Crypto-asset regulatory and supervisory approaches and current practices in Europe. Financial Stability Institute.

Chapter 7: "Evolving Together: Industry Collaboration"

- Young, D. R. (2016). The art of community organizing: Exploring diverse pathways to sustainable and resilient local food systems. Agriculture and Human Values, 33(3), 615-627.

- Maffett, M. (2018). Financial Statement Comparability and the Efficiency of Acquisition Decisions. Journal of Accounting Research, 56(4), 1237-1275.

- Australian Securities and Investments Commission (ASIC). (2020). Digital finance advisory committee report: September 2020.

Conclusion:

- Tapscott, D., & Tapscott, A. (2016). Blockchain revolution: how the technology behind bitcoin is changing money, business, and the world. Penguin.
- Beck, R., Müller-Bloch, C., & Winkler, J. K. (2018). Governance in the Blockchain Economy: A Framework and Research Agenda. Journal of the Association for Information Systems, 19(10), 1072-1093.
- World Economic Forum. (2021). Advancing blockchain governance: Framework and toolkit.

www.ingramcontent.com/pod-product-compliance
Lightning Source LLC
LaVergne TN
LVHW010334070526
838199LV00065B/5748